SAVEUR
ITALIAN
COMFORT FOOD

THE EDITORS OF SAVEUR

TABLE OF CONTENTS

INTRODUCTION

What is comfort food? It is food that gives us both pleasure and a sense of ease—a plate of something nice that delivers well-being along with sustenance.

For many Americans even those of us who didn't grow up with a *nonna* who folded her own *agnolotti* or lingered over a bubbling pot of meat sauce for the Sunday family *pranzo*—the language of comfort food is largely Italian.

A go-to weeknight pasta, a simple assemblage of peak-season tomatoes, torn basil, and fresh mozzarella, the one-pot roast with polenta on the side—these are the gifts of home-style Italian cooking. We value them for their familiarity, their endless variety, their tireless flexibility—and for the ample comfort we find in the bottom of a bowl of pillow-light gnocchi and rich ragù.

In the following pages, you'll find easy takes on such classics as bruschetta and meatballs as well as bigger projects like a whole *porchetta* and a pizza with butternut squash and smoked mozzarella—all of them worth investigating. We've traveled up and down the boot to bring you these satisfying dishes from the Italian kitchen that stir the appetite and taste like home, no matter where your home may be.

Adam

ADAM SACHS
SAVEUR EDITOR-IN-CHIEF

STARTERS

Bruschetta (from the Roman dialect verb *bruscare,* "to toast, burn") is believed to have originated in central Italy, where locals would toast stale bread over hot coals, rub it with garlic, and then use it to sample freshly pressed olive oil. Here, briny olives liven up a classic topping of tomatoes and basil.

TOMATO BRUSCHETTA WITH OLIVES & BASIL

1 cup pitted kalamata olives, finely chopped

½ cup extra-virgin olive oil, plus more for drizzling

¼ cup finely chopped fresh basil

4 ripe tomatoes, cored and diced

Kosher salt and freshly ground black pepper, to taste

1 12-oz. loaf ciabatta, sliced ½" thick on the bias

1 clove garlic, halved lengthwise

SERVES 6

Combine olives, ⅓ cup oil, basil, tomatoes, salt, and pepper in a bowl and set aside. Heat a cast-iron grill pan over medium-high. Brush bread with remaining oil. Grill bread, flipping once, until crisp and slightly charred on edges, about 5 minutes. Transfer bread to a cutting board and rub with garlic. Top with tomato mixture and drizzle with oil to serve.

APERITIVI

The term *aperitivi* refers to beverages designed to stimulate both the appetite and the predinner gathering at which Italians most frequently enjoy them. Typically herbaceous and citrusy, these drinks are almost always bitter and dry and are usually served with small bites to prepare the stomach for the meal to come. Although any cocktail can serve as an *aperitivo,* these three are staples of the Italian cocktail hour.

AMERICANO Created in the mid-1800s by Gaspare Campari using his eponymous aperitif, the Americano was known as the Milano-Torino until the 20th century, when American tourists took strongly to the quaffable premeal drink. The bitter orange–infused liqueur is joined with equal parts sweet Italian vermouth and club soda and served over ice.

NEGRONI Reputedly named after Count Camillo Negroni, and first poured around 1920, this now-iconic drink evolved from a desire to give the Americano a bit more oomph. Dry gin replaces club soda for a more intense cocktail that can be served up or on the rocks.

APEROL SPRITZ Similar to Campari but lighter and lower in alcohol, Aperol is the star in this Italian *aperitivo* that has become a summery favorite throughout Italy as well as abroad. The vibrant orange liqueur is joined by prosecco (dry Italian sparkling wine) and club soda for a bright, bubbly drink. Other Italian *amari* (herbal liqueurs), such as Montenegro, also make great spritzes when mixed with seltzer or sparkling wine.

In Rome, the arrival of zucchini blossoms coincides with the arrival of summer, so do as the Romans do, and kick off the season with this signature antipasto. Light and airy, with a subtle squash flavor, the flowers deliver a delicate contrast to the salty anchovies in the filling.

FRIED ANCHOVY-STUFFED ZUCCHINI BLOSSOMS

Canola oil, for frying

24 anchovies, drained

24 zucchini blossoms, stamens discarded

1 cup flour

2 tbsp. baking powder

Kosher salt and freshly ground black pepper, to taste

1 12-oz. bottle lager-style beer or seltzer, chilled

MAKES 24

Heat 2″ oil in a 6-qt. saucepan until a deep-fry thermometer reads 375°F. Place 1 anchovy fillet in each blossom and roll lengthwise to encase fillet. Whisk flour, baking powder, salt, and pepper in a bowl; whisk in beer until a batter forms. Working in batches and holding stems, dip blossoms in batter and then fry until golden and crisp, 1–2 minutes. Using a slotted spoon, transfer to paper towels to drain. Season with salt.

SQUASH BLOSSOMS

Squash blossoms, or *fiori di zucca*, can be fried, baked, or eaten raw. The male blossoms are more popular for cooking and can be used with or without their stamens removed. Look for blossoms that are vibrant and fresh, and try to use them as soon as possible after they're picked. Like any flower, they'll gradually wilt and begin to discolor. To maximize their shelf life, rinse in cool water and air-dry, then gently wrap in paper towels and store in a sealed container in the refrigerator.

The spiciness of a good *soppressata* (dry salami) makes it an ideal partner to creamy, fluffy ricotta cheese, with the contrast bringing out the best texture and flavor in each element. If you have time, make the ricotta at home (see sidebar); homemade tends to be sweeter than store-bought.

CROSTINI WITH RICOTTA & SOPPRESSATA

1	12-oz. loaf ciabatta or other peasant-style bread, sliced ½" thick on the bias
¼	cup extra-virgin olive oil
1	clove garlic, halved lengthwise
1–1½	cups homemade (see sidebar) or store-bought ricotta
16–24	⅛"-thick rounds soppressata

SERVES 4-6

Heat a cast-iron grill pan over medium-high. Brush bread with oil. Grill bread, flipping once, until crisp and slightly charred on edges, about 5 minutes. Transfer bread to a cutting board and rub with garlic. Spread about 1 tbsp. ricotta on top of each toasted piece; top with 3–4 rounds soppressata.

HOMEMADE RICOTTA

Ricotta is traditionally made by reheating whey left over from cheese making, but it is easy to make a version of it at home using whole milk and rennet. The latter consists of enzymes that act as a coagulant and that produce the sweet, earthy flavor of old-world ricotta.

To make ricotta at home, combine 4 qt. whole milk and ¾ cup heavy cream in a pot and heat over medium-high, stirring occasionally with a wooden spoon, until an instant-read thermometer inserted in the milk reads 200°F. Skim off any foam from the surface of the milk, then pour it into another pot to speed the cooling. Add 2 tsp. kosher salt, stir until the salt dissolves, and let the milk stand until it cools to 125°F. In a bowl, mix 1 tsp. liquid animal rennet (available online) with ¼ cup cold water and then stir the mixture into the milk. Let the milk stand undisturbed until it has visibly thickened, about 10 minutes.

With a wooden spoon, cut a large X in the coagulated surface of the milk, then stir quickly for 15 to 20 seconds to break up the solids. Using a fine-mesh sieve, slowly stir the milk in one direction around the edge of the pot so that the curds begin to separate from the whey. Continue to stir gently until you have gathered a large mass of curds. In batches, gently scoop the curds into a cheesecloth-lined colander set over a sheet or baking pan. Allow the excess whey to drain from the ricotta for 1 hour. Use the cheese immediately or refrigerate, covered, for up to 3 days.

This crostini topping is popular in Tuscany, where beans are pantry staples. Blanching the broccoli rabe removes its bitterness, transforming the leafy, green-stemmed brassica into the ideal companion for the vibrant flavors of the other ingredients.

CROSTINI WITH BROCCOLI RABE, CANNELLINI BEANS & RICOTTA

- 1   12-oz. loaf country bread, sliced ½″ thick on the bias
- ¾   cup extra-virgin olive oil, plus more for drizzling
- 7   cloves garlic (1 halved lengthwise, 6 finely chopped)

     Kosher salt and freshly ground black pepper, to taste

- 2   bunches broccoli rabe, tough stems trimmed
- 2   tsp. chile flakes

     Grated zest of 1 lemon

- 2   tbsp. finely chopped fresh rosemary
- 1   15-oz. can cannellini beans, drained and rinsed
- 2   cups homemade (see sidebar opposite) or store-bought ricotta

SERVES 8

1 Heat oven to 350°F. Place bread on a baking sheet and drizzle with ¼ cup oil; bake, flipping once, until toasted, 20–25 minutes. Transfer bread to a cutting board and rub with halved garlic clove.

2 In a large pot of salted boiling water, cook broccoli rabe until crisp-tender, 2–3 minutes. Drain and squeeze dry, then coarsely chop. Heat ¼ cup oil, half of the chopped garlic, and the chile flakes in a 12″ skillet over medium-high; cook until garlic is soft, 1–2 minutes. Add broccoli rabe, salt, and pepper; cook, stirring occasionally, until golden, 6–8 minutes. Stir in lemon zest and transfer to a bowl.

3 Wipe skillet clean. Heat remaining oil and chopped garlic, plus the rosemary, over medium-high until garlic is soft, 1–2 minutes. Add beans, salt, and pepper; cook, stirring occasionally, until beans are warmed through and slightly toasted, 5–7 minutes.

4 To serve, spread ricotta over each bread slice. Top with broccoli rabe and cannellini beans. Drizzle with more oil and season with salt and pepper.

Butcher shops in Sicily sell these pancetta-wrapped scallions, called *cipollate con pancetta*. Pancetta is often considered "Italian bacon" because, like bacon, it is made from pork belly and is cured, but it is not smoked. Make this snack with either bacon or pancetta.

PANCETTA-WRAPPED SCALLIONS

24   large scallions, trimmed

8   slices pancetta or bacon

Kosher salt and freshly ground black pepper, to taste

¼   cup canola oil

SERVES 4

Wrap 3 scallions together with 1 strip of pancetta. Repeat with remaining scallions and pancetta; season with salt and pepper. Heat oil in a 12″ skillet over medium-high. Working in batches, add pancetta-wrapped scallion bunches and cook, turning as needed, until browned and crisp on all sides, 6–8 minutes. Serve hot.

Thyme and white wine bring out the sweet flavor of mussels in this popular *cicchetto,* one of the many signature snacks made famous in Venetian wine bars and served alongside *aperitivi* (page 15).

STUFFED MUSSELS

30	mussels, steamed open
¾	cup white wine
¼	cup extra-virgin olive oil
⅓	cup grated Parmigiano-Reggiano
¼	cup fresh bread crumbs
6	tbsp. unsalted butter, melted
3	tbsp. fresh thyme leaves
	Kosher salt and freshly ground black pepper, to taste
1	tomato, seeded and finely chopped

SERVES 4-6

Heat broiler to high. Remove and discard top shells from mussels; transfer mussels to a rimmed baking sheet. Drizzle wine and oil over mussels. Combine Parmigiano, bread crumbs, butter, thyme, salt, and pepper in a bowl and divide among mussels. Broil mussels until stuffing is golden brown, about 2 minutes. Serve warm, drizzled with pan juices and topped with tomato.

CICCHETTI: VENETIAN SNACK CULTURE

Cicchetti are a Venetian specialty of handheld bites and colorful plated foods meant to be eaten between meals but especially after work hours in bars and restaurants along the city's bustling canals and sidewalks. They pair particularly well with the region's wines and "spritz" cocktails (a favorite is prosecco and soda tinted orange with Aperol) and are often enjoyed as satisfying snacks before a proper dinner at home.

Delicately seasoned rice croquettes; lightly fried and then marinated sardines with a sweet-sour relish of caramelized onions; sea scallops on the half shell cooked under a blanket of bread crumbs and butter—these are just a few of the plates that stem from the old tradition of enjoying small bites while imbibing or doing business in the city. Similar to Spanish tapas or Greek mezes, the dishes can

be as simple as a bowl of olives or wedges of cheese pierced with toothpicks, or as complex as rehydrated, simmered, and puréed salt cod whipped with olive oil until light and airy and served with radicchio on grilled polenta rectangles (page 39). Other favorites include *insalata di polpo,* or marinated octopus, bright with parsley and lemon juice, and a host of fried foods, from battered zucchini and

mozzarella sandwiches to tiny soft-shell crabs called *moleche*—frying being an ideal way to prepare foods that will be kept at room temperature on the bar.

The tasty dishes cost just a few euros each, but they speak volumes about Venice's rich history as a culinary crossroads and citywide trattoria.

The addition of grated mozzarella and Grana Padano in the ricotta mixture lends these fritters texture and a welcome shot of saltiness. You can make the mixture up to two days in advance and keep it in the refrigerator, or form it into balls and freeze until you're ready to fry.

RICOTTA FRITTERS WITH TOMATO SAUCE

FOR THE SAUCE

2   tbsp. extra-virgin olive oil

4   cloves garlic, crushed

½   tsp. chile flakes

1   14-oz. can crushed tomatoes

6   fresh basil leaves, torn in half

Kosher salt and freshly ground black pepper, to taste

FOR THE FRITTERS

4   oz. thinly sliced prosciutto, finely chopped

1   cup fresh bread crumbs

1   cup homemade (page 18) or store-bought ricotta

½   cup grated Grana Padano

⅓   cup grated mozzarella

1   tsp. finely chopped fresh flat-leaf parsley

½   tsp. grated lemon zest

⅛   tsp. freshly grated nutmeg

3   egg yolks, plus 2 whole eggs

Kosher salt and freshly ground black pepper, to taste

¼   cup flour

½   cup dried bread crumbs (page 33)

Canola oil, for frying

MAKES 20

1 Make the sauce: Heat oil in a 2-qt. saucepan over medium-high. Add garlic and cook, stirring occasionally, until golden, about 5 minutes. Add chile flakes and toast for 1 minute. Add tomatoes and basil, bring to a boil, lower heat to medium, and cook, stirring occasionally, until sauce begins to thicken, 6–8 minutes. Season with salt and pepper. Reduce heat to low and keep sauce warm.

2 Make the fritters: Combine prosciutto, fresh bread crumbs, ricotta, Grana Padano, mozzarella, parsley, lemon zest, nutmeg, egg yolks, salt, and pepper in a medium bowl. Cover and refrigerate until firm, about 30 minutes.

3 Put flour, whole eggs, and dried bread crumbs into 3 separate shallow dishes; whisk eggs. Using your hands, form chilled ricotta mixture into 1½" balls. Working with 1 ball at a time, dredge in flour, dip in eggs, then coat with bread crumbs, shaking off excess. Transfer to a parchment paper–lined baking sheet.

4 Heat 2" canola oil in a 4-qt. saucepan until a deep-fry thermometer reads 350°F. Working in batches, fry ricotta balls, turning occasionally, until golden brown, about 3 minutes. Using a slotted spoon, transfer balls to paper towels to drain. Serve with tomato sauce.

This savory, comforting snack—deep-fried, ragù-filled rice balls—is beloved throughout Sicily. Saffron, which gives the rice a distinctive yellow-orange color, is a reflection of an early culinary influence on the island by the Arabs, who ruled there during the 10th and 11th centuries.

FRIED STUFFED RICE BALLS

3   tbsp. extra-virgin olive oil

½   rib celery, finely chopped

½   small carrot, peeled and finely chopped

½   small yellow onion, finely chopped

3   oz. ground beef

3   oz. ground pork

1   cup tomato sauce

2   tsp. tomato paste

1   small red onion, finely chopped

1½   cups Arborio rice

¼   tsp. crushed saffron threads

2   tbsp. grated Parmigiano-Reggiano

    Kosher salt and freshly ground black pepper, to taste

¼   cup flour

2   eggs

2   cups dried bread crumbs (page 33)

    Canola oil, for frying

MAKES 24

1 Heat 1 tbsp. oil in a 12″ skillet over medium-high. Add celery, carrot, and onion and cook, stirring often, until soft, about 10 minutes. Add beef and pork; cook, stirring often, until browned, 10–12 minutes. Stir in tomato sauce and paste; reduce heat to medium-low and cook, stirring occasionally, until thickened, 45–50 minutes. Transfer meat filling to a bowl and let cool.

2 Heat remaining oil in a 2-qt. saucepan over medium-high. Add red onion and cook, stirring, until soft, about 10 minutes. Add rice and stir to coat. Stir in saffron and 1½ cups water. Bring to a boil, cover, and remove from heat. Let sit for 20 minutes. Remove lid and stir in Parmigiano, salt, and pepper. Spread rice out on a plate and let cool. Meanwhile, whisk together flour, eggs, and ½ cup water in a shallow bowl until smooth. Place bread crumbs in another bowl and set both aside.

3 To assemble, place 1 heaping tablespoon of rice in the palm of your hand and flatten into a disc. Place 1 tsp. cooled meat filling in center of rice disc and form rice around filling to encase it completely; press gently to form a ball. Roll ball in batter and then in bread crumbs until evenly coated. Transfer to a parchment paper–lined baking sheet. Repeat with remaining rice, meat filling, batter, and bread crumbs. Refrigerate for 20 minutes to firm up.

4 Heat 2″ canola oil in a 6-qt. saucepan until a deep-fry thermometer reads 360°F. Working in batches, add rice balls to oil and fry until golden and heated through, about 3 minutes. Using a slotted spoon, transfer rice balls to paper towels to drain. Let cool for 5 minutes before serving.

This recipe comes from Pizzeria Starita, a Neapolitan institution where *pizzaioli* have been sliding pies into the wood-fired oven since 1901. A creamy béchamel binds the fritter filling, which is then chilled to make it easier to cut before it is battered and fried.

HAM & SMOKED MOZZARELLA FRITTERS

10	tbsp. unsalted butter, plus more for greasing
1½	cups flour
5	cups heavy cream
	Kosher salt and freshly ground black pepper, to taste
1	lb. spaghetti
8	oz. smoked mozzarella, cut into ¼″ pieces
4	oz. cooked Italian ham, cut into ¼″ pieces
	Canola oil, for frying
2	cups dried bread crumbs (page 33)

MAKES 30

1 Melt butter in a 1-qt. saucepan over medium-high. Add ½ cup flour and cook, stirring, 2 minutes. Add cream and bring to a boil. Reduce heat to medium and cook until thickened, 4–5 minutes. Set aside.

2 Grease a 9″x 13″ baking dish. Bring a large pot of salted water to a boil. Cook pasta until al dente, about 8 minutes. Drain and transfer to a bowl. Add reserved sauce, mozzarella, ham, salt, and pepper; mix until combined. Press pasta mixture into baking dish. Cover with plastic wrap and refrigerate until firm, about 1½ hours.

3 Heat 2″ canola oil in a 6-qt. saucepan until a deep-fry thermometer reads 325°F. Whisk remaining flour with 1 cup water to form a batter. Put bread crumbs in a bowl. Using a 2″ round cutter, cut 30 rounds out of pasta mixture. Dip rounds in batter and roll in bread crumbs. Fry until golden and crisp, 2–3 minutes. Using a slotted spoon, transfer to paper towels to drain. Serve hot.

These small round peppers are stuffed with canned tuna and anchovies and then preserved in oil. The tart, vibrant flavors of the filling nicely balance the sweet heat of the peppers.

STUFFED CHERRY PEPPERS

5   oz. canned tuna
    in olive oil, drained

8   anchovies, drained if in oil

1½ cups extra-virgin olive oil

¼   cup dried bread crumbs
    (page 33)

2   tbsp. capers, finely chopped

2   tbsp. finely chopped
    fresh flat-leaf parsley

    Kosher salt and freshly
    ground black pepper, to taste

1   32-oz. jar hot red cherry
    peppers, drained, rinsed,
    and stemmed (jar reserved)

SERVES 10–12

Finely chop tuna and anchovies. Combine with ⅓ cup oil, bread crumbs, capers, parsley, salt, and pepper in a bowl. Stuff each pepper with tuna mixture. Transfer to reserved jar; pour remaining oil over peppers. Chill for at least 8 hours to marinate.

TINNED FISH

Italian cooks know the secret to whipping up a fast meal is a well-stocked pantry, and that means a ready supply of not only tuna but also sardines and anchovies. The best and most flavorful are packed in olive oil, salt, or both, contain no added ingredients, and are sourced from Italy, Spain, Portugal, or Morocco. Sardines and anchovies are loaded with protein, calcium, and omega-3 fatty acids, and their oily pungency adds an incredible savory note to a variety of dishes.

SARDINES When it's too hot to cook, do what the Italians do: Layer tomato slices, red onion slices, and chopped parsley with a tin's worth of sardines and dress with black pepper, salt, fresh oregano, and extra-virgin olive oil.

ANCHOVIES A staple of southern Italy, anchovies are typically eaten on crostini with some good olive oil and a squeeze of lemon; arranged atop pizza; or tossed in a basil, olive, and tomato salad. When added to sauces, such as *puttanesca*, they break down, imparting an element of umami to the dish.

Pungent *robiola* cheese hails from the regions of Piedmont and Lombardy. As it warms to room temperature, the cheese begins to slump and its sharp flavors come into focus, making it the perfect foil for sweet accompaniments. Other soft cheeses, such as Brie or ricotta, can be substituted in this easy no-cook appetizer.

ROBIOLA-STUFFED FIGS

1 pint figs (about 15), stemmed

8 oz. robiola cheese, rind removed, at room temperature

2 tbsp. honey

   Kosher salt and freshly ground black pepper, to taste

2 tbsp. pomegranate seeds

   Fresh dill sprigs, to garnish

MAKES 15

Working from the stem end of each fig and using a paring knife, cut an X about halfway toward base; set aside. Combine robiola, honey, salt, and pepper in a bowl. Spoon filling into a piping bag with a plain ½″ tip and pipe about 1 tsp. into each fig. Garnish each fig with pomegranate seeds and dill sprigs.

FIGS

The ancient Romans believed figs, or *fichi*, imported from Greece were superior to those grown on local trees, but today Italians are happy with their own harvest. They eat the plump, rich fruits with prosciutto, bake them into breads, mix them with nuts and honey for cookies, or, as in the recipe here, stuff them with soft, rich cheese for a beautiful and simple antipasto.

This recipe comes from the picturesque town of Sorrento, which sits near citrus groves south of Naples on the Amalfi coast and is famed for the production of the lemon liqueur *limoncello*. Use the freshest lemon leaves available for this dish (look for them at farmers' markets). The heat from the grill will release their fragrance, which is then drawn into the soft mozzarella.

MOZZARELLA WITH GRILLED LEMON LEAVES

4   slices fresh mozzarella, 3–4″ wide and ½″ thick

Kosher salt and freshly ground pepper, to taste

8   large fresh lemon leaves

Extra-virgin olive oil, for drizzling

1   lemon, quartered, to garnish

SERVES 4

Build a medium-hot fire in a charcoal grill, or heat a gas grill to medium. (Alternatively, heat a cast-iron grill pan over medium-high.) Season mozzarella with salt and pepper. Sandwich each slice between 2 lemon leaves and grill until cheese just begins to lose its shape, about 45 seconds. Carefully turn over and grill for 45 seconds more. Transfer to a serving platter, drizzle with oil, and garnish with lemon quarters. Serve immediately.

Though this recipe comes from Abruzzo, it uses the large, bright green olives known as Castelvetranos, which are grown farther south, in Sicily. They are ideal for stuffing, as their mild buttery flavor won't overwhelm the savory filling.

FRIED STUFFED OLIVES

12 oz. Castelvetrano olives (about 40)

3 oz. ground beef

2 oz. ground pork

2 tbsp. grated Parmigiano-Reggiano

¼ tsp. freshly grated nutmeg

1 egg yolk, plus 1 whole egg

Grated zest of 1 lemon

Kosher salt and freshly ground black pepper, to taste

Canola oil, for frying

2 tbsp. milk

1½ cups dried bread crumbs (see sidebar)

½ cup flour

SERVES 4–6

1 Pit olives by lightly crushing each with the flat side of a chef's knife; discard pit, leaving olive as intact as possible. Combine beef, pork, Parmigiano, nutmeg, egg yolk, lemon zest, salt, and pepper in a bowl. Divide mixture into forty ½-tsp. balls. Stuff 1 meat mixture ball into each olive; press olive around filling to seal.

2 Heat 2″ oil in a 4-qt. saucepan until a deep-fry thermometer reads 375°F. Whisk whole egg and milk in a bowl. Put bread crumbs and flour in separate bowls. Working in batches, roll olives in flour, dip in egg mixture, and coat in bread crumbs; fry until crisp and cooked through, 3–4 minutes. Using a slotted spoon, transfer olives to paper towels to drain. Season with salt.

HOMEMADE BREAD CRUMBS

The best bread crumbs are made from a slightly stale loaf of coarse country bread. To make dried bread crumbs, trim the loaf of its crusts and process in a food processor to form crumbs. Dry the crumbs on a baking sheet in a 325°F oven for about 15 minutes; let cool. Process again until fine, and continue baking, stirring once or twice, until pale gold, about 15 minutes. Alternatively, you can make coarse bread crumbs by omitting the second round of processing.

This has to be one of the simplest ways to put your own, sophisticated spin on a cocktail snack. Rosemary and orange is a classic pairing, but you can swap in almost any herb, depending on your preference and what you have on hand.

DRY-CURED OLIVES WITH ROSEMARY & ORANGE

1   orange

1   lb. dry-cured black olives

Leaves from 1 large sprig fresh rosemary, coarsely chopped

Freshly ground black pepper, to taste

SERVES 6-8

Wash orange thoroughly and dry. Using a vegetable peeler, remove zest from orange, taking care to peel as little of the white pith as possible. Coarsely chop zest and transfer to a bowl. Juice orange and add juice to zest along with olives, rosemary, and pepper; toss to coat. Let sit at room temperature for 1 hour to marinate before serving.

OLIVE VARIETIES

The five primary types of Italian olives are *moraioli* and *correggiolo* (the two predominant ones), *frantoio* (from the Italian word for "olive mill"), plump *leccino*, and *pendolino*. Whether picked ripe when purple-black, fully ripened and deep black, cured in brine or salt, or preserved in oil, vinegar, or brine—olives are well loved throughout Italy as a savory snack to enjoy on their own or as part of more complex dishes.

These sweet-and-sour *cicchetti* are a legacy of Venice's seafaring tradition. Sardines were traditionally fried and then marinated with onions in vinegar to preserve them for long sea journeys. Over time, they became a staple at the city's *bacari,* or wine bars, where they could sit on the counter without risk of spoiling.

SWEET & SOUR SARDINES

½ cup white wine

¼ cup raisins

2 lb. fresh sardines, cleaned

Kosher salt and freshly ground black pepper, to taste

¾ cup extra-virgin olive oil

1 large white onion, thinly sliced

⅓ cup white wine vinegar

¼ cup pine nuts

SERVES 6

1 Combine wine and raisins in a bowl. Soak for 30 minutes; drain and set aside. Meanwhile, heat broiler to high. Season sardines with salt and pepper on a baking sheet. Broil until cooked, about 2 minutes; cool.

2 Heat oil in a 4-qt. pan over medium-high. Add onion and cook until browned, 10–12 minutes. Add vinegar, reduce heat to medium-low, and cook until onion is soft, 6–8 minutes. Stir in reserved raisins, pine nuts, salt, and pepper; let cool.

3 Place half of sardines on bottom of an 8″ x 8″ dish; cover with half of onion. Place remaining sardines on top; cover with remaining onion. Chill for 4 hours to marinate.

Made with ground veal and potatoes, these crisp fried balls are a classic Italian snack. To keep the interior of the *crocchette* soft and tender, do not overwork the meat mixture before shaping it into balls.

VEAL CROCCHETTE

½ cup milk

2 slices white sandwich bread

1½ lb. ground veal or pork

2 cups mashed potatoes

⅔ cup finely chopped fresh flat-leaf parsley

8 eggs

2 cloves garlic, finely chopped

Kosher salt and freshly ground black pepper, to taste

Canola oil, for frying

½ cup flour

1 cup dried bread crumbs (page 33)

MAKES 30

1 Pour milk over bread in a bowl and let soak for 10 minutes. Squeeze bread to drain milk; discard milk. Place bread in a bowl and combine with veal, potatoes, parsley, 4 eggs, garlic, salt, and pepper. Shape mixture into about thirty 1″ balls; place on a parchment paper–lined baking sheet and chill for at least 1 hour.

2 Heat 2″ oil in a 6-qt. saucepan until a deep-fry thermometer reads 350°F. Place flour, remaining eggs, and bread crumbs in 3 separate bowls. Whisk eggs. Working in batches, dredge each meatball in flour, dip in eggs, and coat in bread crumbs. Fry until golden brown, about 5 minutes. Using a slotted spoon, transfer to paper towels to drain.

If you travel to Italy and go to a local bar for an *aperitivo* and snack, you might come across this codfish mousse (*mantecato* means "whipped") served on toast or a slice of baguette, but purists serve it atop a rectangle of grilled polenta. One bite and you'll know why: The combination of charred cornmeal cake with the fluffy, salty spread can't be beat.

BACCALÀ MANTECATO

10 oz. dried salt cod

4 cups milk

1 clove garlic, crushed

1 rib celery, halved

1 yellow onion, halved

½ cup extra-virgin olive oil, plus more for brushing

Kosher salt and freshly ground black pepper, to taste

1⅓ cups quick-cooking polenta

18 small leaves radicchio

2 tbsp. finely chopped fresh flat-leaf parsley

SERVES 10–12

1 Place cod in a 2-qt. saucepan and cover with 2" cold water; bring to a boil and cook for 20 minutes. Drain cod, return to saucepan, and repeat process twice more. Transfer cod to a 6-qt. saucepan and add milk, garlic, celery, onion, and 10 cups water; bring to a boil. Reduce heat to medium-low and cook until cod is tender, about 20 minutes. Drain cod, reserving ¼ cup cooking liquid; discard vegetables and skin and bones from cod. Process cod and reserved cooking liquid in a food processor until smooth. With the motor running, slowly drizzle in oil until emulsified; continue mixing until smooth. Transfer to a bowl and season with salt and pepper; chill.

2 Meanwhile, bring 4 cups salted water to a boil in a 4-qt. saucepan. While whisking, add polenta and cook, stirring, until thick, 3–5 minutes. Transfer to a greased 9" x 12" rimmed baking sheet; smooth top and chill until set.

3 Heat a cast-iron grill pan over high. Cut polenta into eighteen 2" x 3" rectangles; brush with oil. Working in batches, grill polenta, turning once, until slightly charred, about 4 minutes. Top each rectangle with a radicchio leaf and a dollop of cod mousse; sprinkle with parsley.

POLENTA

Polenta, or cornmeal, has long been a cornerstone of northern Italian home cooking. Traditionally, it was prepared over an open fire in a copper pot, or *paiolo*, with a long wooden spoon, or *tarello*. It called for constant stirring until the cornmeal and water thickened into a golden mass, at which point the polenta was poured out onto a wooden board for serving. Today, the mixture of grain and water still demands almost constant stirring, so making polenta calls for considerable patience and elbow grease (though some very good instant polentas are available these days). The grain is available in yellow or white and finely or coarsely textured, but most Italians favor the yellow coarse-grind cornmeal for its chewy texture and hearty taste that barely hints of sweet corn.

SOFT & CREAMY Butter and Parmigiano-Reggiano or Gorgonzola can be stirred into polenta for a rich side dish. Serve it as an accompaniment to game birds and roasted meats or use it as a cushion for ragù, stewed meats, seafood, or vegetables.

COOLED & FIRM Cool polenta in a pan, then slice and grill it and serve as an appetizer topped with sautéed mushrooms or other savory tidbits; slice, layer with cheese, tomato sauce, or other ingredients, and bake in the oven; or cut into thin sticks and deep-fry.

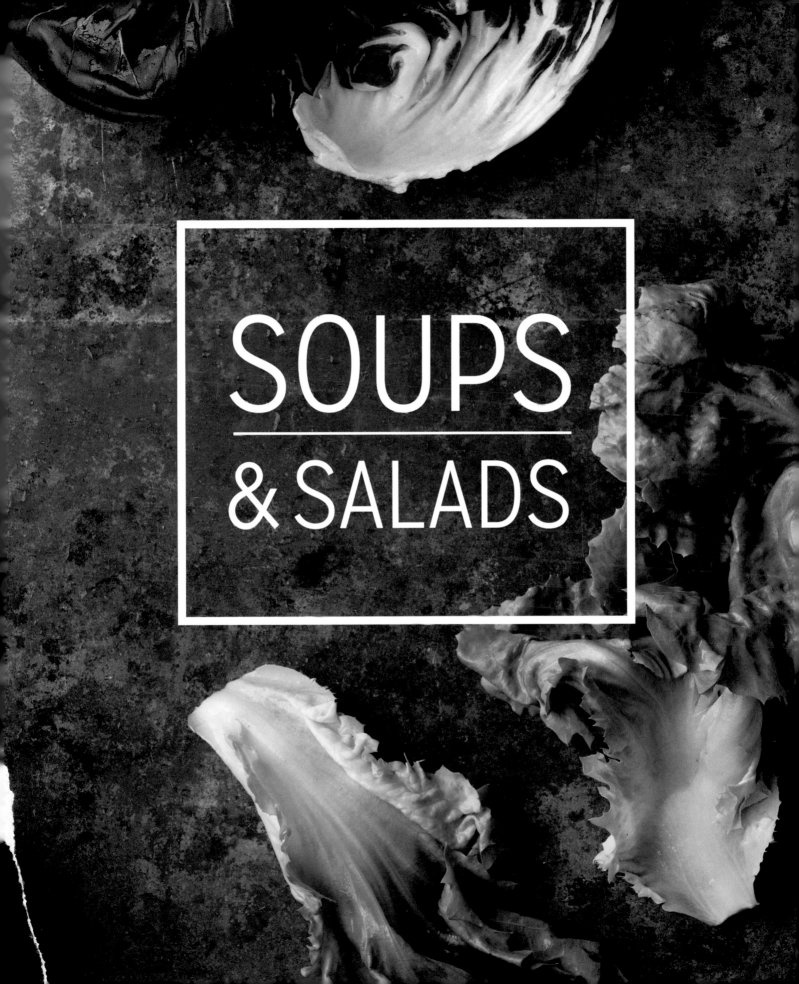

SOUPS
& SALADS

In Italy, spring's arrival is often celebrated by serving *vignole,* a hearty Roman-style vegetable soup. In this version, we substitute bacon for the standard pancetta and add ground veal. Use the freshest vegetables the season has to offer—such as peas and fava beans—and add a squeeze of lemon juice to each bowl to brighten the flavors.

SPRING VEGETABLE SOUP

¼ cup extra-virgin olive oil

6 oz. ground veal

4 slices bacon, diced

1 yellow onion, finely chopped

2 carrots, peeled and diced

4 cups chicken stock

1 cup shelled and peeled fava beans (about 1 lb. unshelled beans)

½ cup fresh or frozen peas

Kosher salt and freshly ground black pepper, to taste

Grated Parmigiano-Reggiano, for serving

Lemon wedges, for serving

SERVES 4

Heat oil in a 4-qt. saucepan over medium-high. Add veal, bacon, and onion. Cook, stirring occasionally, until veal is cooked and bacon has rendered its fat, 6–8 minutes. Add carrots and cook until soft, 5 minutes more. Add stock and simmer for 10 minutes. Add favas, peas, salt, and pepper and cook 3–5 minutes longer. Ladle soup into bowls and serve with Parmigiano and lemon wedges on the side.

Some Italians argue that French onion soup was actually invented in Tuscany and then introduced at the French court by Catherine de Médici in the 1500s. In this take on that Renaissance recipe, a combination of cipollini and red onions imparts a deep, natural sweetness.

TUSCAN ONION SOUP

½ cup extra-virgin olive oil

1 lb. cipollini onions, thinly sliced

1 lb. red onions, thinly sliced

6 cups beef stock

Kosher salt and freshly ground black pepper, to taste

4 slices country-style bread, toasted

1½ cups grated Grana Padano

SERVES 4

1 Heat oil in a 6-qt. saucepan over medium-low. Add cipollini and red onions and cook, stirring occasionally, until caramelized, 30–35 minutes. Add stock and simmer 30 minutes more. Season with salt and pepper.

2 Heat oven to 400°F. Divide bread between 4 ovenproof serving bowls; pour soup over each slice of bread and sprinkle each with 6 tbsp. Grana Padano. Bake until cheese is golden and bubbling, 5–7 minutes. Serve immediately.

This is one of Tuscany's most famous culinary improvisations: An attempt to stretch classic minestrone soup by adding bread resulted in a brand-new classic. When freshly made, this is a hearty yet brothy soup; when reheated the next day, it thickens to a flavorful, porridge-like stew. Zolfini beans, a pale yellow heirloom variety, may be hard to find; cannellini beans make a fine substitute.

TWICE-COOKED TUSCAN BREAD SOUP

1	lb. dried zolfini or cannellini beans, soaked overnight and drained
10	tbsp. extra-virgin olive oil
4–5	fresh sage leaves
3–4	whole black peppercorns
2	cloves garlic, crushed
	Kosher salt and freshly ground black pepper, to taste
2	yellow onions, chopped
1	cup canned chopped Italian plum tomatoes
2	carrots, peeled and thickly sliced
2	potatoes, peeled and thickly sliced
2	ribs celery, thickly sliced
1	bunch cavolo nero (lacinato) kale, coarsely chopped
1	bunch Swiss chard, coarsely chopped
½	small Savoy cabbage, cored and coarsely chopped
3	thick slices day-old country bread

SERVES 6, TWICE

1 Combine beans, 2 tbsp. oil, the sage, peppercorns, garlic, and 12 cups water in an 8-qt. saucepan and bring to a boil. Reduce heat to medium and simmer, covered, for 1 hour. Season to taste with salt, reduce heat to medium-low, and gently simmer, stirring occasionally, until beans are tender, 1–2 hours more. Drain, reserving cooking liquid and 1 cup beans. Purée remaining beans with 2 cups cooking liquid.

2 Heat 4 tbsp. oil in an 8-qt. saucepan over medium-low. Add onions and cook until soft, about 20 minutes. Add tomatoes, carrots, potatoes, celery, kale, chard, and cabbage, stirring until combined; cover and cook until greens wilt, about 20 minutes. Add puréed beans and remaining cooking liquid. Simmer, covered, until vegetables are soft, about 1 hour. Add bread and reserved beans; cover, and cook until bread begins to soften, about 10 minutes. Season with salt and pepper and serve. Refrigerate leftover soup.

3 The next day, heat oven to 375°F. Heat leftover soup in a casserole dish, uncovered, stirring occasionally, until heated through, about 1 hour. For the last 30 minutes, do not stir; let soup brown lightly. Drizzle with remaining oil and serve.

Known as *pappa al pomodoro,* this thick soup calls for day-old bread. Once it has broken down, it adds body and balances the acidity of the tomatoes. If you don't have stale bread, dry out slices of fresh bread in a 250°F oven for about 20 minutes before adding them to the soup.

BREAD & TOMATO SOUP

½ cup extra-virgin olive oil

2 cloves garlic, finely chopped

2 leeks, white and light green parts only, rinsed and finely chopped

9 cups puréed peeled Italian tomatoes or canned tomato purée

1½ cups chicken stock

1½ cups beef stock

9 ¾"-thick slices stale unsalted Tuscan bread (about 1 lb.), halved

2 tbsp. chopped fresh basil leaves

Kosher salt and freshly ground black pepper, to taste

SERVES 6-8

1 Heat ⅓ cup oil in a 6-qt. saucepan over medium. Add garlic and cook until light golden, about 2 minutes. Reduce heat to medium-low, add leeks, and cook, stirring often, until very soft, 15–20 minutes. Add tomatoes and stocks and bring to a boil over high. Reduce heat to medium and simmer, stirring occasionally, for 30 minutes.

2 Remove pot from heat. Add bread, pushing it into soup with a wooden spoon until each piece is submerged. Add basil and stir gently to combine. Cover and set aside to let bread soak until completely softened, about 30 minutes. Uncover pot and whisk soup vigorously until bread breaks down and soup resembles porridge, 4–5 minutes. Season with salt and pepper. Gently reheat soup over medium. Ladle soup into warm bowls and drizzle with remaining oil.

BEAN BASICS

Legumes were the ultimate comfort food in Roman times, and they remain an essential element in modern Italian cuisine. From Tuscany's classic bean soup made with creamy white cannellini beans to the famous green lentils of Umbria, no region is lacking in iterations of favorite *minestre* and *paste e fagioli*.

"Beans are the meat of the poor man," wrote Pellegrino Artusi, author of the Italian classic *Science in the Kitchen and the Art of Eating Well*. It is certainly true that beans were a major player in *la cucina povera*, infusing protein into the diet of the poor while stifling hunger pangs and providing affordable and nutritious sustenance. Today, they are an integral component of the canon of Italian cuisine, beginning with the fresh harvest in June, when markets overflow with brilliantly hued varieties sold shelled or still nestled in their pods. Fresh beans, sometimes labeled "shelling beans" or "shell beans" in the United States, are available for only a short time. The rest of the year, cooks rely on dried or canned beans, although dried beans have superior flavor and are more economical.

Cooking techniques are simple, with certain key points to keep in mind. After soaking dried beans in water overnight, drain them, add water to cover by at least 3 inches, bring to a boil, and then simmer until the beans are tender but not mushy, usually about an hour, depending on the variety. Fresh beans don't need to be soaked and will cook in about 20 minutes. Italians like to add peppercorns, garlic cloves, and fresh sage leaves to the cooking water, but don't salt the beans before they are done or they will toughen. Save the fragrant bean broth to add to a vegetable soup.

Here are the most popular varieties of beans in Italian cuisine.

CANNELLINI Sometimes called white kidney beans, cannellini beans are the backbone of such Tuscan staples as *ribollita, fagioli all'uccelletto*, and the sublimely simple mix of cannellini, garlic, sage, and peppery olive oil. Along with a mildly nutty and earthy flavor, they have a creaminess that adds texture to soups and braises.

BORLOTTI Known in the United States as cranberry beans, these marbled white-and-pink legumes are favored for the Venetian take on *pasta e fagioli*, perhaps the most classic of all Italian bean soups. They have a somewhat thick skin and a desirable meaty quality that holds up well during cooking.

LENTILS Although you'll find lots of lentil varieties in the best markets, look for Italy's famed Castelluccio lentils. Varying in hue from pale green to dark brown, they have a thin skin and soft texture attributed to the climate and soil of the mountainous area in Umbria where they are cultivated. They cook quickly, and the nutty flavor pairs beautifully when simmered with pork sausages.

CHICKPEAS Known as *ceci* in Italy, these ancient beans are a staple in households from the central peninsula down through the south and beyond. The toothsome legume will fit in anywhere other beans go: added to pasta swathed in a light tomato sauce, tossed with tuna and sweet white onions, or in a hearty soup, where its mellow sweetness will shine through.

FAVAS Before Columbus's voyages to the New World, the fava, or broad bean, was the staple bean in Europe, where it had been consumed for thousands of years. Favas are harvested in April, and fresh beans are available until about June. As with so many Italian vegetables, favas are best prepared simply, most notably as the Romans do, in a pan sauté that includes pancetta and onion.

Here is simple, hearty Italian cooking at its best. To serve this rustic soup in the traditional manner, place a slice or two of toasted country-style bread that has been rubbed with garlic and drizzled with olive oil on the bottom of each bowl and then ladle the soup over the top.

BEAN SOUP WITH SQUASH & KALE

2 cups dried cannellini beans, soaked overnight and drained

2 carrots, peeled and coarsely chopped

1 rib celery, coarsely chopped

½ yellow onion, coarsely chopped

¾ cup extra-virgin olive oil

4 cloves garlic (3 finely chopped, 1 halved)

10 oz. winter squash, such as butternut, peeled, seeded, and cut into ½" cubes (about 2 cups)

4 large kale leaves, preferably cavolo nero (lacinato), stemmed and chopped

1 waxy potato, peeled and cut into ½" cubes

Kosher salt and freshly ground black pepper, to taste

½ tsp. crushed fennel seeds

8 thick slices country-style bread

SERVES 4–6

1 Combine beans, half of carrots, the celery, onion, and 5 cups water in a 4-qt. saucepan; bring to a boil and reduce heat to medium-low. Simmer, covered, until beans are tender, 40–45 minutes. Set ¾ cup beans aside; transfer remaining beans and their cooking liquid to a blender and purée. Set puréed beans aside.

2 Heat 2 tbsp. oil in a 6-qt. pot over medium. Add finely chopped garlic and cook, stirring often, until soft, about 3 minutes. Add reserved bean purée along with remaining carrots, the squash, kale, potato, and 1 cup water. Season with salt and pepper, bring to a boil, and reduce heat to medium-low; cook, covered, until vegetables are tender, about 20 minutes. Stir in fennel seed and reserved whole beans. Meanwhile, toast bread and rub with halved garlic clove; drizzle each toast with 1 tbsp. oil. To serve, place 1 to 2 pieces toasted bread in the bottom of each soup bowl and ladle soup over top. Drizzle soup with remaining oil.

This soup—full of vegetables, chickpeas, and pasta—is a meal in itself. If the dish stands for a while rather than being served immediately, the pasta will continue to absorb the liquid and transform the soup into a thick stew. To return the stew to a thinner, more souplike consistency, add more stock and reheat gently.

CHICKPEA & CAVATELLI SOUP

3   tbsp. extra-virgin olive oil

2   ribs celery, coarsely chopped

1   carrot, peeled and coarsely chopped

1   small yellow onion, coarsely chopped

Leaves from 3 sprigs fresh rosemary, finely chopped

6   cups vegetable stock

1   15-oz. can chickpeas, drained and rinsed

8   oz. cavatelli

Kosher salt and freshly ground black pepper, to taste

2   tbsp. finely chopped fresh flat-leaf parsley

Grated Parmigiano-Reggiano, for serving

SERVES 4-6

Heat oil in a 6-qt. saucepan over medium-high. Add celery, carrot, onion, and rosemary and cook until soft, 8–10 minutes. Add stock and chickpeas and simmer for 5 minutes. Remove half of chickpeas and purée until smooth; return chickpeas to pan. Add pasta and cook until al dente, 10 minutes. Season with salt and pepper. Serve with parsley and Parmigiano sprinkled on top.

Cacciucco, which means "mixture," is a centuries-old seafood stew that originated in the port city of Livorno and traditionally used "bottom-of-the-boat" fish—those left behind after the more desirable fish had been sold. Our version, with its six types of fish and shellfish, evokes that colorful image. For more on octopus, see page 61.

CACCIUCCO

6	tbsp. extra-virgin olive oil
1	tbsp. finely chopped fresh flat-leaf parsley
1	tbsp. finely chopped fresh sage
½	tsp. chile flakes
5	cloves garlic (4 finely chopped, 1 halved)
12	oz. baby octopus, cleaned and cut into 1″ pieces
12	oz. calamari, cleaned and cut into 1″ pieces
1	tbsp. tomato paste
1	cup white wine
1	14-oz. can chopped tomatoes
	Kosher salt and freshly ground black pepper, to taste
1	cup fish stock
1	1-lb. monkfish fillet, cut into 2″ pieces
1	1-lb. red snapper fillet, cut into 2″ pieces
12	oz. large shell-on shrimp
12	oz. mussels, scrubbed and debearded
8	1″-thick slices country-style white bread

SERVES 6–8

1 Heat ¼ cup oil in a 6-qt. saucepan over medium. Add parsley, sage, chile flakes, and finely chopped garlic and cook until fragrant, about 1 minute. Add octopus and calamari and cook, stirring occasionally, until opaque, about 4 minutes. Add tomato paste and cook until paste has darkened slightly, about 1 minute. Add wine and cook, stirring often, until the liquid has evaporated, about 20 minutes. Add tomatoes, salt, and pepper and cook, stirring occasionally, until seafood is tender, about 10 minutes. Stir in stock and simmer, covered, for 10 minutes. Add monkfish and cook, covered, until just firm, about 5 minutes. Add snapper and shrimp and scatter mussels over top. Cook, covered, without stirring, until snapper is just cooked through and mussels have just opened, about 10 minutes; discard any mussels that failed to open.

2 Meanwhile, heat oven to 375°F. Brush bread with remaining oil and bake, flipping once, until golden and toasted, 20 minutes. Rub with halved garlic clove. Serve stew over bread or with bread on the side.

Typically made during the winter holidays with day-old bread or bread sticks, this cheese soup-stew from northern Italy is filling and satisfying, the ultimate comfort food on a cold night.

CHEESE & BREAD SOUP

3½	cups beef or chicken stock
5	tbsp. unsalted butter
10	oz. Italian bread sticks
1	lb. Taleggio cheese, sliced
	Kosher salt and freshly ground black pepper, to taste
½	small onion, thinly sliced

SERVES 8-10

1 Bring stock to a boil in a saucepan and remove from heat. Grease bottom of a 3-qt. high-sided skillet with 1 tbsp. butter. Break bread sticks into 2½″ pieces. Put 1 layer of bread sticks in skillet. Cover bread sticks with a layer of cheese. Continue layering bread sticks and cheese. Ladle stock over bread sticks one ladleful at a time and heat skillet over low heat. Bring to a simmer and cook, without stirring, for 30 minutes. Season with salt and pepper.

2 Meanwhile, melt remaining butter in a 12″ skillet over medium heat. Add onion and cook until onion is soft, 8–10 minutes. Strain butter and onion through a fine-mesh sieve, pressing on onion with back of a spoon; discard onion. Drizzle butter over soup and continue cooking for 10 more minutes before serving.

A traditional *panzanella,* or Tuscan bread salad, calls for moistening stale bread with water before combining it with the other ingredients and the dressing. This twist on the classic ensures that the bread retains some of its crispness by having it tossed in just before serving.

MUSHROOM, TOMATO & MOZZARELLA BREAD SALAD

½   cup extra-virgin olive oil

4   tbsp. unsalted butter

½   lb. porcini mushrooms, quartered

3   cloves garlic, sliced

Half a baguette or other good bread, torn into ½" cubes (about 6 oz.)

2   tbsp. balsamic vinegar

4   large heirloom tomatoes (about 2 lb.), cored and sliced into ¼" wedges

Kosher salt and freshly ground black pepper, to taste

5   oz. fresh mozzarella, cut into 1" pieces

1   handful fresh basil leaves, thinly sliced, plus sprigs to garnish

SERVES 4

1 Heat oven to 350°F. Heat ¼ cup oil and the butter in a 12" ovenproof skillet over medium. When butter has melted, remove skillet from heat and add mushrooms, garlic, and bread cubes; mix well. Place skillet in oven and bake until bread cubes are golden and crisp, 20–25 minutes. Remove skillet from oven and set aside to cool.

2 Gently toss remaining oil, the vinegar, tomatoes, salt, and pepper in a large bowl.

3 Shortly before serving, toss bread mixture, tomatoes, mozzarella, and sliced basil in a large bowl. Transfer salad to a serving platter and garnish with basil sprigs.

Sugar-sweet green *radicchio zuccherino* is found only on the island of Istria and in northeastern Italy; a good substitute is mâche (lamb's lettuce). This simple yet bold salad comes from Lidia Bastianich, who adds garlic in thick slices so the garlic-shy can pick it out easily. "If you don't mind the garlic, chop it finely," she says.

MÂCHE & EGG SALAD

6 cups mâche or radicchio zuccherino

2 tbsp. extra-virgin olive oil

1½ tbsp. red wine vinegar

3 cloves garlic, thickly sliced

Kosher salt and freshly ground black pepper, to taste

2 hard-cooked eggs, peeled and quartered

Toss mâche, oil, vinegar, garlic, salt, and pepper in a large bowl. Add eggs, then toss gently one more time. Serve garnished with pepper.

SERVES 6

WHAT IS "EVOO"?

Extra-virgin olive oil. Most cooks would say they know what this pantry staple is. But much misunderstanding and misinformation surround this popular ingredient.

To be labeled "extra virgin," olive oil must be produced in a specified manner and meet certain chemical and taste standards. Carefully picked olives must be crushed by purely mechanical means within 24 hours of harvesting, and the acidity level of the oil that results must be less than 0.8 percent. But these are only the minimum requirements. A panel of certified tasters must then verify that the oil has positive taste attributes, such as fruitiness, and that it contains no chemical or off-putting aromas or flavors.

Because extra virgin is the highest grade of olive oil, it's the best choice for most culinary uses. The harsh waxiness of virgin olive oil, even if used only for frying or marinades, can affect the taste of food. Instead, for deep frying particularly, use neutral-tasting canola or sunflower oil.

But despite the high standards it indicates, the extra-virgin label isn't a guarantee of quality or best flavor. (One study found that 69 percent of imported extra-virgin olive oil didn't meet acceptable taste standards because of fraudulent labeling or oxidation during shipping.) Try to sample the oil before you buy it. This is both a quality check and a way to find the oil that best suits your taste.

Olive oil is like wine: Its taste is dependent on the variety of olives used, the way the olives were grown, when they were picked, and a number of other factors. Each region, each farm, and each batch will be different, so taste a spoonful. Let the oil roll around in your mouth to coat your taste buds and release the aroma. Pick out the flavor notes of pepper, fruit, herbs, and grass. Consider the consistency and mouthfeel and go with the one you like best.

Fried briny capers and sweet basil leaves punch up the flavor in this adaptation of the classic *insalata caprese* from the island of Capri in the Gulf of Naples. Use caution when frying the basil, as it has a tendency to cause spattering when submerged in hot oil.

CAPRESE SALAD WITH FRIED BASIL & CAPERS

⅓ cup extra-virgin olive oil, plus more for drizzling

¼ cup capers, drained and patted dry

12 fresh basil leaves

8 oz. fresh mozzarella, sliced ¼″ thick

3 vine-ripened tomatoes, cored and sliced ¼″ thick

Kosher salt and freshly ground black pepper, to taste

Balsamic vinegar, for drizzling

SERVES 4-6

1 Heat oil in a 4-qt. saucepan over medium-high. Cook capers until crisp, 6–8 minutes. Using a slotted spoon, transfer capers to paper towels to drain. Working in batches, fry basil leaves until crisp, about 30 seconds, and transfer to paper towels to drain.

2 To serve, arrange mozzarella slices and tomatoes in an alternating pattern on a serving plate. Tuck fried basil pieces between tomato and mozzarella slices, season to taste with salt and pepper, and scatter with fried capers. Drizzle with oil and vinegar.

BUFFALO MOZZARELLA VS BURRATA

Mozzarella di bufala and burrata are both traditional Italian fresh cheeses made from the milk of the water buffalo and shaped into balls of varying sizes. Burrata however, goes a step further. Burrata is created when the balls are stuffed with a mixture of soft, unfinished mozzarella curds and cream, an invention dating from the 1920s in Puglia.

There are large herds of indigenous Italian water buffalo in Italy, especially in the area of Campania in southern Italy where they are raised for milk production. For centuries their milk has been used to make fresh mozzarella cheese. In 1996, *Mozzarella di Bufala de Campana* was awarded the European Union's Protected Designation of Origin or PDO.

Fresh mozzarella from water buffalo milk is highly regarded for its earthy, slightly bittersweet flavor and soft but sliceable texture. Burrata, because of its lush stuffing of cream and soft curd, is unctuous and extra-rich in flavor, and when sliced, the center oozes slightly. The cheeses can be used interchangeably in caprese salad and also pair well with prosciutto or fresh figs.

Fresh mozzarella and burrata are also made from cow's milk, but these are considered to be less-flavorful versions of the traditional cheese made with buffalo milk.

Octopus is popular along Italy's Mediterranean and Adriatic coasts, where it often appears in simply prepared salads. Here, the texture of the firm yet tender octopus contrasts with the creaminess of the potatoes, but both take well to the vinegar and olive oil that bind the salad together.

OCTOPUS & POTATO SALAD

2   lb. octopus, cleaned

2   bay leaves

1   wine cork

1   shallot, thinly sliced

1   lb. multicolored
     baby potatoes

     Kosher salt and freshly
     ground black pepper,
     to taste

¼   cup extra-virgin olive oil

3   tbsp. red wine vinegar

3   tbsp. roughly chopped
     fresh flat-leaf parsley

SERVES 4–6

1 Put octopus, bay leaves, and cork in a 6-qt. saucepan; cover with water and bring to a boil. Reduce heat and simmer until tender, 30–45 minutes; drain. Remove bay leaves and cork. Let cool, then cut octopus into 1" pieces and set aside.

2 Soak shallot in cold water for 10 minutes, then drain. Meanwhile, put potatoes in a pot of generously salted water and bring to a boil. Lower heat and simmer until potatoes are tender, 15 minutes; drain and cool slightly. Lightly smash potatoes with your fingers, then toss with octopus, shallot, oil, vinegar, parsley, salt, and pepper.

WORKING WITH OCTOPUS

Octopus is a beloved ingredient in coastal Italy, owing to its proliferation in the Mediterranean waters. In Venice, it comes marinated in a bright chile-and-lemon dressing, and Sicilian cooks simmer it in a garlicky tomato sauce. In Tuscany, it forms the backbone, along with mussels and shrimp, of *cacciucco*, a classic seafood stew (page 52). Cooks in the United States are less familiar with octopus, however, which can make it intimidating to prepare. But with some help from your fishmonger and a few tips, that doesn't have to be the case.

When buying fresh octopus, ask the fishmonger to remove both the head and the beak. Once they're gone, you're left with a ring of tentacles. Rinse the tentacles thoroughly to remove any grit or sand and place them in a pot large enough to accommodate them with plenty of room to spare. Cover the tentacles with water, bring them to a gentle simmer, and let them bubble away until a paring knife inserted into the thickest part of a tentacle pierces it with ease. This can take anywhere from 30 minutes to an hour or more, depending on the size of the octopus. Many Italian cooks insist on placing a cork in the cooking water. They believe the natural enzymes in the cork help tenderize this creature of the deep, though others have found that octopus cooks to perfect tenderness without the cork.

Once the octopus is done, drain it and allow it to cool. If the skin and suckers are unappealing to you, peel them off and discard them. Cut the tentacles into bite-size pieces for use in a salad, or grill the whole tentacles quickly to char the outside lightly, then serve with lemon wedges.

One of Sicily's most famous dishes, *caponata* is a relish-like eggplant salad with an *agrodolce*—"sour-sweet"—flavor (page 169). Numerous versions of this salad are found on the island, many of which include seafood. Here, tuna, a Sicilian pantry staple, is added.

SICILIAN EGGPLANT & TUNA SALAD

¾ cup extra-virgin olive oil

2 eggplants, peeled and cut into small cubes

3 ribs celery, chopped

1 yellow onion, chopped

Kosher salt and freshly ground black pepper, to taste

1 tomato, coarsely chopped (optional)

¼ cup red wine vinegar

1 tbsp. sugar

¾ cup capers, drained

1 tbsp. pine nuts

1 6-oz. can oil-packed tuna, drained and broken up with a fork

Leaves from ½ bunch fresh flat-leaf parsley, finely chopped

1 Heat oil in a 12″ skillet over medium-high. Add eggplant and cook until golden, about 10 minutes. Using a slotted spoon, transfer eggplant to a bowl. Reduce heat to medium-low, add celery, onion, salt, and pepper and cook, covered and stirring occasionally, until vegetables are soft, about 15 minutes. Add tomato, if using, to skillet. Cover skillet and cook 10 minutes more. Return eggplant and its juices to skillet.

2 Stir vinegar and sugar in a small saucepan over medium until sugar dissolves, about 1 minute, then add to skillet. Add capers and pine nuts to skillet; cover and cook 5 minutes more. Remove skillet from heat and set aside to cool, then mix in tuna and parsley. Serve slightly warm or at room temperature.

SERVES 8

Raisins give a sweet pop to this salad from the wine regions of central Italy. Rehydrated in warm water so they're plump and soft, they create a nice counterpoint to the crunch and freshness of the arugula, pears, and pine nuts.

ARUGULA WITH PECORINO, PEARS & RAISINS

1 cup boiling water

3 tbsp. raisins

1 tbsp. fresh lemon juice

2 ripe pears, peeled, cored, and thinly sliced

5 oz. baby arugula

Kosher salt and freshly ground black pepper, to taste

4 oz. chunk Pecorino Romano

3 tbsp. pine nuts, toasted

¼ cup balsamic vinegar

½ cup extra-virgin olive oil

SERVES 4

Combine water and raisins in a bowl; let sit for 20 minutes, then drain. Toss lemon juice with pears in a bowl. Arrange arugula on a serving platter and season with salt and pepper. Top with pears and shave Pecorino over top. Sprinkle with raisins and pine nuts. Whisk vinegar, salt, and pepper in a bowl. While whisking, slowly drizzle in oil until emulsified. Drizzle dressing over salad.

This classic Sicilian salad takes advantage of the citrus that flourishes on many parts of the island. Blood oranges bring sweetness and a dramatic color to the plate, and their zest adds a welcome tartness to the mix of shrimp and fennel.

SHRIMP & FENNEL SALAD

1 large bulb fennel (about 1 lb.), trimmed and thinly sliced, fronds reserved to garnish

¼ cup extra-virgin olive oil

8 oz. large shrimp, peeled and deveined, tails on (about 24)

Kosher salt and freshly ground black pepper, to taste

2 blood oranges, zested, peeled, seeded, and supremed (page 67), juices reserved

½ cup fresh flat-leaf parsley leaves

SERVES 4

Soak fennel in cold water for 10 minutes; drain and set aside. Heat 2 tbsp. oil in a 12″ skillet. Add shrimp, season with salt and pepper, and cook, turning once, until evenly pink and cooked through, 3 minutes. Cool slightly, then toss with fennel, remaining oil, the blood orange zest, segments, and juice, the parsley, salt, and pepper. Garnish with reserved fennel fronds.

FENNEL: THE WHOLE VEGETABLE

Fennel is one of the Mediterranean's oldest crops. With its bright green and feathery leaves, anise-flavored bulb, and aromatic seeds, fennel is also one of the most versatile ingredients. There are three distinct parts of the fennel plant, and all are edible.

FRONDS Also known as leaves, the fronds make a beautiful garnish to salads, soups, and fish dishes.

BULB Known in Italian as the *finocchio*, the white bulbous body adds a strong flavor, similar to licorice, and can be consumed raw or cooked. Raw fennel adds great crunch to salads, as in the recipe at left.

SEEDS The seeds, known as the herb fennel seed, are an essential ingredient in many *salumi* (cured meats) and fresh sausages, in some biscotti, and in other preparations.

Blood oranges, which are available from December through April, form the basis of this refreshing citrus salad. Serve it tossed or as a composed salad, which allows diners to appreciate the beauty of the crimson orange slices.

BLOOD ORANGE & RED ONION SALAD

3–4 blood oranges
1 small red onion, thinly sliced
  Kosher salt and freshly ground black pepper, to taste
2 tbsp. extra-virgin olive oil

SERVES 4

Peel oranges, removing pith with a paring knife. Cut oranges into ¼"-thick slices and arrange on a serving platter. Spread onion over oranges. Season with salt and pepper and drizzle with oil.

SUPREMING CITRUS

Supreming is a technique used on citrus to remove the membrane and pith, so that only the sweetest, juiciest part of the fruit is reserved. If you like, try it with this recipe instead of cutting the oranges into rounds.

1 Cut off the ends of the fruit: Using a chef's knife, cut a thin slice from the top and bottom of the fruit to expose the flesh.

2 Cut away the peel and pith: Stand the fruit on a cutting board on a flat end. Following the curve of the fruit, cut away all the peel and white pith. Continue in this fashion, working your way around the fruit.

3 Trim any remaining pith: Trim off any leftover white pith using the tip of the knife.

4 Release the segments: Working over a bowl, make a cut on both sides of each segment to free it from the membrane, letting the segment and juice drop into the bowl below.

Made with farro, an ancient grain with a chewy texture and rich, nutty flavor, this hearty salad can be the centerpiece of a meal or served as a side dish. Mix in additional seasonal vegetables, if you like, and if serving as a main course, accompany with country-style bread.

FARRO SALAD WITH FAVA BEANS & RADICCHIO

1	cup farro
2	cups shelled and peeled fava beans (about 2 lb. unshelled beans)
¼	cup extra-virgin olive oil
3	tbsp. red wine vinegar
1	shallot, finely chopped
	Kosher salt and freshly ground black pepper, to taste
½	cup shaved Pecorino Romano, plus more to garnish
½	head radicchio, thinly sliced

SERVES 4

1 Combine farro and 5 cups water in a 4-qt. saucepan and bring to a boil. Reduce heat and simmer until farro is tender, 45 minutes. Add fava beans and cook for 3 minutes; drain, then run under cold water until cool.

2 Meanwhile, whisk oil, vinegar, shallot, salt, and pepper in a large bowl until combined. Add farro and fava beans, Pecorino, and radicchio and toss to combine. Transfer to a serving platter and garnish with more Pecorino.

Puntarelle is a bitter winter chicory grown in the countryside around Rome. To temper its sharp flavor, soak its sturdy shoots in ice-cold water for about an hour. This salad is finished with a sprinkle of slightly sweet, lightly floral bee pollen granules, available at specialty food stores.

PUNTARELLE & DANDELION GREEN SALAD

Grated zest of 1 lemon, plus 3 tbsp. lemon juice

1½ tsp. Dijon mustard

1 tsp. honey

Kosher salt and freshly ground black pepper, to taste

3 tbsp. extra-virgin olive oil

¼ cup Castelvetrano olives, pitted and coarsely chopped

6 oz. dandelion greens, trimmed

4 oz. puntarelle or other chicory, trimmed

½ tsp. bee pollen

SERVES 6

Whisk lemon zest and juice, mustard, honey, salt, and pepper in a large bowl until combined. While whisking, slowly drizzle in oil until vinaigrette is emulsified. Stir in olives. Tear dandelion greens and puntarelle into bite-size pieces and add to bowl. Using your hands, toss greens with vinaigrette, coating leaves completely. Transfer salad to a serving platter or plates and sprinkle with bee pollen.

CHICORIES

Chicories are a diverse group of greens—though they are often white and purple as well—that are widely grown in Italy and play a key role in many regional dishes. Prized for their crunch and bitterness, they complement richer ingredients like nuts and sweet fruits, as well as fish, poultry, and sharp cheeses.

RADICCHIO With striking purple leaves accented with white veins, radicchio comes in many varieties in Italy, most notably the round, cabbage-like Chioggia and the narrow, almond-shaped Treviso. They all have a characteristic bitter spiciness that mellows with cooking. Radicchio is typically drizzled with olive oil and grilled or tossed into pastas or salads.

PUNTARELLE The spindly outer leaves and thick, asparagus-like core distinguish this farmers' market favorite from other, more widely available chicories. The cores are sliced lengthwise into thin strips and then typically crisped in ice water, drained, and tossed with an anchovy dressing to balance the bitterness.

ESCAROLE Leafier and somewhat less bitter than its brethren, escarole is a welcome element in salads—it looks like a head of curly lettuce—as well as in soups, stews, and pastas, where it holds its shape even after a long cook.

PASTA
RISOTTO
& PIZZA

This trio of gnocchi (here and on pages 76 and 79) are from Portland chef Jenn Louis, by way of her extensive travels in Italy. In this Umbrian dish, fennel pollen in the ragù adds a sweet aroma and a flavor reminiscent of the fennel-laced sausages sold in Italian butcher shops. The addition of farro flour to the dough results in gnocchi that are slightly denser than those made with all-purpose flour.

FARRO GNOCCHI WITH PORK RAGÙ

FOR THE RAGÙ

- 2 tbsp. extra-virgin olive oil
- 1 lb. ground pork
- 2 slices bacon, finely chopped
- ½ tsp. chile flakes
- ½ tsp. fennel pollen
- 1 clove garlic, thinly sliced
- ¼ cup tomato paste
- ⅓ cup dry red wine
- 5 cups chicken stock
  Kosher salt, to taste
- 4 tbsp. unsalted butter
- 1 cup finely grated Parmigiano-Reggiano, plus more for serving
- ¼ cup chopped fresh flat-leaf parsley

FOR THE GNOCCHI

- 1¾ lb. Yukon gold potatoes, scrubbed
- 1½ cups all-purpose flour, plus more for dusting
- ¾ cup farro flour
- 1 cup plus 1 tbsp. finely grated Parmigiano-Reggiano
- 2 eggs, lightly beaten
  Semolina flour, for dusting

SERVES 6

1 Make the ragù: Heat oil in a 6-qt. saucepan over medium-high. Cook pork and bacon until browned, 4–5 minutes. Add chile flakes, fennel pollen, and garlic and cook until garlic is golden, 2–3 minutes. Stir in tomato paste and cook for 2 minutes. Add wine and cook until evaporated, about 30 seconds. Add 4 cups stock and season with salt; bring to a boil. Reduce heat to medium; simmer until thickened, about 1 hour.

2 Make the gnocchi: Add potatoes to a 4-qt. saucepan of boiling water. Reduce heat to medium-high and simmer until potatoes are tender, 25–30 minutes; drain. When potatoes are cool enough to handle, peel and pass through a potato ricer into a bowl. Add flours, Parmigiano, and eggs; using your hands, mix until a soft dough forms. Transfer dough to a lightly floured surface and knead until smooth. Cover dough with plastic wrap and let sit at room temperature for 30 minutes.

3 Quarter dough and, working with one quarter at a time, use your hands to roll dough into a ½"-thick rope. Cut rope crosswise into 1" gnocchi. Transfer gnocchi to a semolina-dusted parchment paper–lined baking sheet. Separate gnocchi to prevent sticking.

4 In a large pot of generously salted boiling water, cook gnocchi, all at once, until they float, 2–3 minutes. Using a slotted spoon, transfer gnocchi to a parchment paper–lined baking sheet; keep warm.

5 Return ragù to medium heat. Add remaining stock and the butter; simmer until sauce is thickened, 6–8 minutes. Add cooked gnocchi and the Parmigiano; cook until warmed through, 1–2 minutes. Divide gnocchi and sauce between shallow bowls. Garnish with more Parmigiano and parsley.

Buckwheat flour gives these gnocchi an earthy flavor that pairs perfectly with a springtime sauce starring peas and spinach. As the seasons change, try different vegetables, like zucchini or other thin-skinned squash in the summer and roasted butternut squash in the fall.

BUCKWHEAT & RICOTTA GNOCCHI

FOR THE GNOCCHI

1¾	cups plus 2 tbsp. homemade (page 18) or store-bought ricotta
½	cup finely grated Pecorino Romano
2	tsp. kosher salt, plus more to taste
½	tsp. freshly grated nutmeg
¼	tsp. freshly ground black pepper, plus more to taste
4	egg yolks
1	cup plus 3 tbsp. all-purpose flour, plus more for dusting
¾	cup plus 2 tbsp. buckwheat flour
	Semolina flour, for dusting

FOR THE SAUCE

1	cup fresh or frozen peas
1⅓	cups heavy cream
4	oz. baby spinach
¾	cup finely grated Parmigiano-Reggiano
1	tbsp. fresh lemon juice

SERVES 6-8

1 Make the gnocchi: Stir ricotta, Pecorino, salt, ¼ tsp. nutmeg, pepper, and egg yolks in a bowl until smooth. Add flours and, using your hands, mix until a slightly firm dough forms. Quarter dough and cover loosely with plastic wrap. On a lightly floured surface, and working with ¼ of dough at a time, use your hands to roll dough into a ½″-thick rope. Cut rope crosswise into ¼″ gnocchi. Transfer gnocchi to a semolina-dusted parchment paper–lined baking sheet. Separate gnocchi to prevent sticking.

2 Make the sauce: In a large pot of generously salted boiling water, cook gnocchi, all at once, until they float, 2–3 minutes. About halfway through cooking gnocchi, add peas to pot. Meanwhile, bring cream to a simmer in a 12″ skillet over medium-high. Stir in remaining nutmeg. Using a slotted spoon, transfer gnocchi and peas to skillet with cream. Stir in spinach, ½ cup Parmigiano, the lemon juice, salt, and pepper. If sauce is too thick, add ⅓ cup water from cooking gnocchi. Divide gnocchi between plates; garnish with remaining Parmigiano.

Classic gnocchi contain just flour and potato, but in this recipe from chef Jenn Louis, adding ricotta and eggs to the dough results in a richer, smoother, more luxurious dumpling. Olives, capers, and Grana Padano flavor the slowly simmered tomato sauce that dresses this ultimate comfort food.

RICOTTA GNOCCHI WITH OLIVES, CAPERS & TOMATOES

FOR THE GNOCCHI

2	lb. Yukon gold potatoes, scrubbed
1⅔	cups flour, plus more for dusting
7	tbsp. homemade (page 18) or store-bought ricotta
2	tsp. kosher salt
2	eggs, lightly beaten

FOR THE SAUCE

2	tbsp. extra-virgin olive oil, plus more for drizzling
½	tsp. chile flakes
4	cloves garlic, finely chopped
1	bay leaf
1	yellow onion, finely chopped
1	sprig fresh rosemary
6	tbsp. cold unsalted butter, cubed
2	28-oz. cans whole peeled tomatoes, crushed by hand
	Kosher salt and freshly ground black pepper, to taste
¾	cup green Castelvetrano or Gaeta olives, pitted and halved
⅓	cup finely grated Grana Padano, plus more for serving
¼	cup capers, drained, rinsed, and coarsely chopped
2	tbsp. coarsely chopped fresh oregano

SERVES 6

1 Make the gnocchi: Add potatoes to a 4-qt. saucepan of boiling water. Reduce heat to medium-high and simmer until potatoes are tender, 25–30 minutes; drain. When potatoes are cool enough to handle, peel and pass through a potato ricer into a bowl. Add flour, ricotta, salt, and eggs; using your hands, mix until a smooth dough forms. If dough is sticky, add more flour 1 tbsp. at a time as needed. Transfer dough to a lightly floured surface and quarter. Working with one quarter at a time, use your hands to roll dough into a ¾"-thick rope. Cut rope crosswise into 1" gnocchi. Transfer gnocchi to a flour-dusted parchment paper–lined baking sheet. Separate gnocchi to prevent sticking. Cover with plastic wrap; chill until ready to cook.

2 Make the sauce: Heat oil in a 6-qt. saucepan over medium and cook chile flakes, garlic, bay leaf, onion, and rosemary until vegetables are soft, 6–8 minutes. Add butter, tomatoes, and salt; simmer until thickened, about 1½ hours. Discard bay leaf and rosemary; keep sauce warm. Stir olives, Grana Padano, capers, and oregano into sauce.

3 In a large pot of generously salted boiling water, cook gnocchi, all at once, until they float, 2–3 minutes. Using a slotted spoon, transfer gnocchi to sauce; season with salt and pepper and stir to combine. Divide gnocchi between serving bowls; drizzle with oil and sprinkle with Grana Padano.

REGIONAL SAUCES

If there's one thing the many regions of Italy have in common, it's a love of pasta. The style of saucing varies from place to place, and each sauce has evolved from unique customs and local produce. Here are some well-known regional sauces.

ABRUZZO While Abruzzo is often overlooked as a source of popular Italian cuisine, some believe that *carbonara*, a style of saucing with eggs, pancetta, and cheese, originated here among charcoal workers, or *carbonari*, before being popularized in Rome. (See page 89.)

CAMPANIA The seaside city of Naples is home to the famous *marinara*, or "mariner's style" sauce, consisting simply of tomatoes, olive oil, oregano, and garlic. And where mariners flocked, so did another sort: *Pasta alla puttanesca* is named for the "ladies of the night" and is distinguished by the addition of capers, olives, anchovies, and chiles.

EMILIA-ROMAGNA The city of Bologna is responsible for the well-known *alla bolognese*, a meat-based tomato sauce with ground beef and fatty pork as well as red wine, celery, and carrots.

LAZIO The Lazio region is home to Italy's capital city, but east of Rome, the town of Amatrice developed a style of saucing called *all'amatriciana* that combines tomato, *guanciale* (cured pork cheek), and crushed red chiles. (See page 102.)

LIGURIA In warm, coastal Genoa, an abundance of basil inspired the verdant green pesto sauce now prized far beyond its origin. The term *pesto* comes from *pestare*, "to pound." Any purée can by definition be a pesto, but *pesto alla genovese*, featuring toasted pine nuts, grated cheese, basil, garlic, and olive oil, is easily the most famous. (See page 97.)

PIEDMONT In Piedmont, adjacent to Switzerland, fresh gnocchi are tossed with *fonduta*, the northern Italians' response to fondue. The style, known as *alla bava* (*bava* means "drooling" or "dribbling," in reference to the melted cheese), combines melted local Fontina, egg yolks, and cream.

SARDINIA Italy's northern island is home to a lesser-known sauce called *alla campidanese*, a sausage-and-tomato ragù that is distinguished from other versions by the addition of saffron threads. It is most often served with *malloreddus*, a ridged dumpling-shaped pasta whose name translates to "young bulls" in the Sardinian dialect.

SICILY Off the toe of the Italian boot, Sicily is home to a local variation on the more widespread basil pesto from Genoa. *Pesto alla trapanese* trades out the pine nuts for almonds and adds fresh tomatoes to the purée (see page 82). The tomato- and eggplant-based *pasta alla Norma*, named after Sicilian-born Vincenzo Bellini's opera *Norma*, is another regional favorite.

TUSCANY Known for a plentiful population of wild boar, Tuscany is home to *pappardelle al sugo di cinghiale*, a pasta served with a rich stewed-meat sauce made from red wine and gamy wild boar.

UMBRIA Norcia, a town in Italy's mountainous central region famous for its annual winter truffle harvest, is responsible for *pasta alla Norcina*, a rich cream-based sauce featuring sausage or anchovies and the town's famed *tartufi neri* (black truffles).

VENETO In Venice, *bìgoli in salsa* is prepared with wholewheat *bigoli* (a long noodle-like spaghetti) and a sauce made from anchovies, onions, and white wine.

Guanciale (cured pork cheek) and a reduction of sagrantino wine flavor the sauce for this creamy dish, a classic of the Umbrian town of Montefalco. Although gnocchi in Italy often have distinctive lines made by pressing the dough against the grooves of a wooden gnocchi paddle, Umbrian gnocchi is traditionally smooth.

GNOCCHI WITH CREAM & RED WINE SAUCE

FOR THE GNOCCHI

- 1   lb. russet potatoes
- 2   tsp. kosher salt, plus more to taste
- 1¼ cups flour, plus more for tossing
- 2   eggs, lightly beaten

FOR THE SAUCE

- 1   tbsp. extra-virgin olive oil
- 1   tbsp. unsalted butter
- 2   oz. guanciale or pancetta, finely chopped
- 1   small yellow onion, thinly sliced
- 1½ cups robust red wine, such as sagrantino
- 1¼ cups heavy cream
     Freshly ground black pepper, to taste
- ½   cup grated Parmigiano-Reggiano, plus more for serving

SERVES 6-8

1 Make the gnocchi: Add potatoes to a 4-qt. saucepan of boiling water. Reduce heat to medium-high and simmer until potatoes are tender, 25–30 minutes; drain. When potatoes are cool enough to handle, peel and pass through a potato ricer into a bowl. Stir in 2 tsp. salt, flour, and eggs until dough forms. Transfer dough to a lightly floured surface; knead until smooth. Divide dough into 6 balls. Working with 1 ball at a time, roll dough into a 20″ rope about ¾″ thick. Cut crosswise into 1″ pieces and transfer to a parchment paper–lined baking sheet. Toss with some flour to prevent sticking. Chill until ready to use.

2 Make the sauce: Heat oil and butter in a 12″ skillet over medium. Cook guanciale until fat renders, 4–6 minutes. Add onion; cook until golden, 8–10 minutes.

Add wine; cook until evaporated, 20–22 minutes. Add cream, salt, and pepper; bring to a boil, then remove from heat. Let sauce cool slightly, then transfer to a blender and purée until smooth; return sauce to skillet and keep warm.

3 Bring a large pot of generously salted water to a boil and, working in batches, cook gnocchi until tender, 4–5 minutes. Using a slotted spoon, transfer gnocchi to skillet with sauce. Stir in ⅓ cup Parmigiano, salt, and pepper. Garnish with remaining Parmigiano.

This dish features a flavorful pesto from Sicily that's made from ingredients common in the region, including spicy chiles, and is traditionally served with homemade *busiate,* a spiral-shaped pasta. If you're pressed for time, dried fusilli can be substituted.

BUSIATE WITH SICILIAN PESTO

FOR THE PESTO

1	pint cherry tomatoes
¾	cup sliced almonds, toasted
½	cup packed fresh basil leaves
½	cup finely grated Parmigiano-Reggiano, plus more for serving
5	tbsp. extra-virgin olive oil
2	tbsp. capers, drained
2	tbsp. golden raisins
¼	tsp. chile flakes
3	anchovies, drained
2	cloves garlic, chopped
1	peperoncini, stemmed, seeded, and coarsely chopped
	Kosher salt and freshly ground black pepper, to taste

FOR THE PASTA

3	cups flour, plus more for dusting
1	tsp. kosher salt
1	tbsp. extra-virgin olive oil
3	eggs, plus 1 egg yolk

SERVES 6-8

1 Make the pesto: Place tomatoes in a food processor and process until finely chopped; pour into a fine-mesh sieve and drain excess juices. Return tomatoes to processor and add almonds, basil, Parmigiano, oil, capers, raisins, chile flakes, anchovies, garlic, and peperoncini; process until finely ground. Season with salt and pepper; chill until needed.

2 Make the pasta: In a large bowl, whisk together flour and salt and form a well in the center. Pour oil, eggs and egg yolk, and 2 tbsp. water in well. Using a fork, slowly stir until flour is incorporated and dough forms. Transfer to a lightly floured surface and knead until smooth, about 8 minutes. Wrap dough in plastic wrap and let rest for 1 hour.

3 Divide dough into 6 equal pieces. Working with 1 piece at a time, roll into a ⅛"-thick rope and cut rope into 2" lengths. Place one end of each length on the end of a wooden skewer and roll on work surface until length wraps around skewer and forms a corkscrew.

4 Bring a large pot of generously salted water to a boil. Working in batches, add pasta and cook, stirring, until al dente, about 8 minutes. Drain, reserving ¼ cup cooking water. Transfer pasta to a large bowl along with pesto. Toss to combine, adding a couple spoonfuls of cooking water, if needed, to create a smooth sauce. Transfer to a large serving platter or bowls and serve with more Parmigiano.

The flavors in this dish are common to southern Italy, where capers and lemon groves abound. Artichokes are so revered here that the small Sicilian town of Cerda, in the province of Palermo, has erected a statue in honor of the *carciofo* ("artichoke"). An annual festival there celebrates the edible thistle.

SPAGHETTI WITH ARTICHOKES, LEMON & CAPERS

¼ cup extra-virgin olive oil

4 cloves garlic, finely chopped

1 small onion, finely chopped

1 tsp. chile flakes

½ cup white wine

1 12-oz. can quartered artichokes, drained

⅓ cup grated Parmigiano-Reggiano, plus more to garnish

Kosher salt and freshly ground black pepper, to taste

1 lb. spaghetti

⅓ cup capers, drained

3 tbsp. finely chopped fresh flat-leaf parsley, plus more to garnish

Grated zest and juice of 1 lemon

SERVES 6-8

1 Heat oil in a 6-qt. saucepan over medium-high. Add garlic, onion, and chile flakes and cook, stirring occasionally, until golden brown, about 10 minutes. Add wine and artichokes and cook until wine is reduced by half, 3 minutes. Stir in Parmigiano and season with salt and pepper. Set aside and keep warm.

2 In a large pot of generously salted boiling water, cook spaghetti, stirring occasionally, until al dente, 8–9 minutes. Drain, reserving ¼ cup cooking water. Add pasta and cooking water to reserved sauce and cook about 5 minutes more. Add capers, parsley, lemon zest and juice, salt, and pepper and toss to combine. Transfer to a platter and garnish with more Parmigiano and parsley.

When most people think of pesto, the traditional Genovese version—made with basil and pine nuts—comes to mind. In this rendition, sweet and nutty *cavolo nero* (also known as lacinato kale or Tuscan kale) replaces both of those ingredients. The pesto is paired with farfalle ("butterflies"), commonly called bow ties.

FARFALLE WITH CAVOLO NERO PESTO

Kosher salt and freshly ground black pepper, to taste

2½   **lb. cavolo nero (lacinato) kale, trimmed**

4   **cloves garlic**

1   **cup extra-virgin olive oil**

1   **tsp. sea salt**

1   **lb. farfalle**

1½   **cups grated Parmigiano-Reggiano**

SERVES 4

1 In a large pot of salted boiling water, cook kale and 2 cloves garlic until kale is bright green, 3–4 minutes; drain. Transfer kale, garlic, and ¼ cup oil to a food processor and purée. Transfer pesto to a large bowl. Crush remaining garlic cloves with sea salt and stir into pesto with ¼ cup oil.

2 In a large pot of generously salted boiling water, cook farfalle until al dente, 10 minutes; drain. Add pasta to bowl of pesto. Fold in Parmigiano, remaining oil, salt, and pepper.

ITALIAN GRATING CHEESES

Hard grating cheeses are a hallmark of Italian cooking. They are added to pastas, gratins, sauces, salads, soups, stews, and more. Sometimes the cheese is incorporated directly into the dish, as with minestrone and lasagna. Other times it tops a dish, as with spaghetti Bolognese. Here are the three most widely used Italian grating cheeses.

PARMIGIANO-REGGIANO An aged cow's milk cheese with a granular texture that has long been made in Emilia-Romagna and a small area of Lombardy, Parmigiano-Reggiano is used for grating and shaving and as a cheese course with fruit and nuts or with aged balsamic vinegar. The flavor of the cheese depends on its age. At 18 months, it has a nutty, somewhat sharp taste; after 24 to 36 months, the flavor is both nutty and spicy. Only wheels labeled "PDO" (protected designation of origin) can legally bear the Parmigiano-Reggiano name.

GRANA PADANO Similar in character to Parmigiano-Reggiano but milder, Grana Padano is made from skimmed cow's milk in five Italian regions: Emilia-Romagna, Lombardy, Piedmont, Trentino, and Veneto. The cheese, which is aged from 9 months to 24 months or more, has a mild, almost sweet flavor that grows more full flavored and complex with time. When the cheese is young, the texture is soft and somewhat crumbly; with age, it becomes much grainier and develops crystalline patches. Like its better-known cousin, Parmigiano-Reggiano, authentic Grana Padano carries a PDO label.

PECORINO Nutty, mild, and soft but crumbly when young and grainy and sharply flavored when mature, pecorino cheese is made from sheep's milk and can be aged from less than a month to more than a year. Pecorino Romano, the best-known of the big pecorino family, is made in Lazio and Sardinia and in Grossetto Province in Tuscany and has PDO status, as do Pecorino Toscano (Tuscany), Pecorino Sardo (Sardinia), Pecorino Siciliano (Sicily), and Pecorino di Filiano (Basilicata). Most pecorinos are sold aged, but Pecorino Toscano, which has a milky taste and buttery texture when young, is both a popular table cheese and grating cheese in its home region.

In central Italy, *pasta alla carbonara*, which roughly translates to "pasta of the charcoal worker," is made with only a few ingredients: raw eggs, grated salty cheese, crispy pancetta (or *guanciale*), and plenty of black pepper. The dish can be enhanced with any number of additions, including earthy porcini mushrooms, a natural partner to pancetta.

SPAGHETTI CARBONARA WITH PORCINI MUSHROOMS

3 tbsp. extra-virgin olive oil

4 cloves garlic, crushed

10 oz. pancetta, cut crosswise into ¼" strips

1½ lb. porcini mushrooms, thinly sliced

⅔ cup white wine

Kosher salt and freshly ground black pepper, to taste

1 lb. spaghetti

⅔ cup finely grated Parmigiano-Reggiano

¼ cup finely grated Pecorino Romano

2 tbsp. finely chopped fresh flat-leaf parsley

2 eggs

SERVES 4

1 Heat oil in a 12" skillet over medium-high. Add garlic and cook until golden, about 1 minute. Remove and discard garlic. Add pancetta and cook until edges are crisp, about 6 minutes. Using a slotted spoon, transfer pancetta to a plate. Add mushrooms to the skillet and cook until golden, 6–8 minutes. Add reserved pancetta and wine and cook until thickened, about 3 minutes. Remove from heat.

2 In a large pot of generously salted boiling water, cook spaghetti until al dente, about 7 minutes. Drain, reserving ¼ cup cooking water. In a large bowl, whisk together Parmigiano, Pecorino, parsley, and eggs; while whisking, slowly drizzle in reserved pasta water until smooth. Add spaghetti along with reserved pancetta mixture. Season with salt and a generous amount of pepper. Toss to combine and serve immediately.

This pasta dish is inspired by the flavors of Calabria, one of the few regions in Italy to feature the heat of chiles as a central hallmark of its cuisine. Fennel, another popular ingredient in the Calabrian kitchen, nicely complements the spiciness.

ZITI WITH SAUSAGE, FENNEL & TOMATOES

¼	cup extra-virgin olive oil
4	cloves garlic, finely chopped
1	small onion, finely chopped
1½	tsp. chile flakes
1	lb. sweet Italian sausage, casings removed
1	bulb fennel (about 8 oz.), trimmed and thinly sliced, fronds reserved to garnish
	Kosher salt and freshly ground black pepper, to taste
1	15-oz. can whole peeled tomatoes, crushed by hand
⅓	cup grated Grana Padano
1	lb. ziti

SERVES 6-8

1 Heat oil in a 6-qt. saucepan over medium-high. Add garlic, onion, and chile flakes and cook, stirring occasionally, until golden brown, about 10 minutes. Add sausage and cook, breaking up meat into small pieces, until browned, 16–18 minutes. Add fennel, season with salt and pepper, and cook until soft, 8–10 minutes. Add tomatoes and bring to a simmer; cook, stirring occasionally, until reduced by a third, 4–5 minutes. Stir in Grana Padano and season with salt and pepper. Set aside and keep warm.

2 In a large pot of generously salted boiling water, cook ziti, stirring occasionally, until al dente, 8–9 minutes. Drain, reserving ¼ cup cooking water. Add pasta and cooking water to reserved sauce and cook about 5 minutes more. Garnish with reserved fennel fronds.

COOKING PERFECT PASTA

The first step in cooking good pasta is to salt the water adequately. You'll want a generous amount, so the water tastes like the sea. The late Marcella Hazan suggested using 1½ tbsp. salt (preferably not iodized, as it will give the pasta a metallic taste) for every 1 lb. of pasta. You can also add salt according to the amount of water, following the general guideline of 1 tbsp. salt for every 2 qt. water.

To ensure the pasta moves freely as it cooks and to avoid clumping, use at least 5 qt. water to cook 1 lb. pasta and stir the pasta often during the first 2–3 minutes of cooking. To determine doneness, start tasting the pasta at least 2 minutes before the package directions indicate. Keep in mind that slightly undercooked or al dente pasta will continue to cook from the residual heat after being drained. Once the pasta is ready, set aside at least 1 cup cooking water before you drain the pasta and use it as needed to adjust the consistency of the sauce. Finally, do not rinse pasta once you have drained it. Sauce adheres to hot pasta better than it does to cool pasta, and the starch that stays on the pasta after it is initially drained can help thicken and bind the sauce.

Unlike the typically heavy red-sauced lasagne served in America, this layered pasta dish from Abruzzo relies on an ethereal, egg-enriched tomato sauce that puffs as the lasagne cooks.

VEAL & SPINACH LASAGNE

FOR THE DOUGH

3 cups flour, plus more for dusting

4 eggs

FOR THE FILLING

3 tbsp. unsalted butter

1 large yellow onion, finely chopped

1½ lb. ground veal

8 oz. spinach, stemmed

¼ tsp. freshly grated nutmeg

Kosher salt and freshly ground black pepper, to taste

FOR THE SAUCE & ASSEMBLY

7 tbsp. cold unsalted butter (5 tbsp. cubed, plus more for greasing)

3 cloves garlic, thinly sliced

1 15-oz. can whole peeled tomatoes, crushed by hand

Kosher salt and freshly ground black pepper, to taste

¾ cup milk

8 eggs

1¼ cups grated Parmigiano-Reggiano

1 lb. fresh mozzarella, thinly sliced

SERVES 8

1 Make the dough: Mound flour on a work surface and make a large well in the center; crack eggs into well. Using a fork, whisk eggs while slowly incorporating flour until dough comes together. Using your hands, knead dough until elastic and smooth, 8–10 minutes. Divide dough in half, flatten into discs, and wrap in plastic wrap. Chill for 30 minutes.

2 Make the filling: Melt 2 tbsp. butter in a 12" skillet over medium-high. Cook onion until golden, 6–8 minutes, and transfer to a bowl. Add remaining butter and the veal and cook, stirring and breaking up meat into small pieces, until browned, 6–8 minutes; transfer to bowl with onion. Add spinach to skillet and cook until wilted, 1–2 minutes; transfer to a colander to drain. Squeeze spinach dry, coarsely chop, and add to bowl with veal. Stir in nutmeg, salt, and pepper

3 Make the sauce: Melt 2 tbsp. butter in a 4-qt. saucepan over medium. Cook garlic until golden, 1–2 minutes. Add tomatoes, salt, and pepper and cook until thickened, 8–10 minutes; let cool. Purée milk and eggs in a blender until smooth. Add tomato mixture, salt, and pepper and pulse 2–3 times until just combined.

4 Cook the lasagne sheets: Bring a large pot of generously salted water to a boil. On a lightly floured work surface and working with 1 disc of dough at a time, press and stretch dough into an 8" oval; dust on both sides with flour. Using a pasta machine, pass dough through machine twice, using the widest setting. Using the next narrower setting, pass dough through machine twice more. Continue to roll dough, setting rollers to the next narrower setting, until dough is 1½" thick. Lay dough sheet on a lightly floured surface and cut into ten 12" sheets. Working in 2 batches, cook lasagne sheets 20–30 seconds. Using a slotted spoon, transfer lasagne sheets to an ice bath.

5 Assemble and bake the lasagne: Heat oven to 375°F. Generously grease a 9" x 13" baking dish with butter. Lay 2 lasagne sheets in prepared dish, overlapping slightly. Sprinkle 1 cup filling over top and drizzle with ½ cup sauce. Sprinkle with ¼ cup Parmigiano and about 3 oz. mozzarella, then dot with 1 tbsp. cubed butter. Repeat 2 more times layering lasagne sheets, filling, sauce, cheeses, and butter. Cover lasagne with greased parchment paper and aluminum foil and bake until filling is set, about 45 minutes. Toward the end of baking, heat broiler. Uncover lasagne and broil until cheese is browned, 2–3 minutes. Serve warm or at room temperature.

Piedmontese cuisine often showcases porcini mushrooms, which are commonly foraged at the base of the Italian Alps. Prized for their meaty texture and nutty flavor, they are most often sold dried in the U.S. Once rehydrated, they regain their texture and toothsomeness.

CORZETTI WITH MUSHROOM RAGÙ

4 oz. dried porcini mushrooms

2 cups boiling water

Kosher salt and freshly ground black pepper, to taste

1 lb. corzetti or orecchiette

¾ cup extra-virgin olive oil

6 cloves garlic, thinly sliced

8 oz. cremini mushrooms, thinly sliced

8 oz. shiitake mushrooms, stemmed and thinly sliced

2 cups veal stock

½ cup grated Parmigiano-Reggiano

¼ cup finely chopped fresh flat-leaf parsley

SERVES 6-8

1 Place porcini in a bowl and cover with water; let sit until softened, about 15 minutes. Using a slotted spoon, transfer porcini to a cutting board and coarsely chop; reserve ½ cup soaking liquid.

2 In a large pot of generously salted boiling water, cook pasta until al dente, about 11 minutes. Drain, reserving ½ cup cooking water. Toss pasta with ¼ cup oil and set aside.

3 Wipe pot dry, add remaining oil and the garlic, and heat over medium-high. Cook until garlic is soft, 1–2 minutes. Add cremini and shiitake mushrooms and cook, stirring occasionally, until golden, 7–9 minutes. Add reserved porcini and reserved soaking liquid, the stock, salt, and pepper and simmer until sauce is slightly reduced, 5–7 minutes. Stir in reserved pasta and cooking water, plus half of Parmigiano and 3 tbsp. parsley. Garnish with remaining Parmigiano and parsley.

CORZETTI STAMP

Corzetti are pasta made and enjoyed throughout Liguria and in southeastern Piedmont. Although you can buy them premade, you can also create this coinlike pasta at home using a special artisanal mold to stamp out each round. The molds were common in the Renaissance and typically bore a coat of arms or a reference to the event for which the pasta was being prepared. Often the design was of a cross, which is probably how the pasta, called *crosetti* or *croxetti* in Emilia-Romagna, got its name. One half of the mold is concave and cuts the pasta; the other half is carved with the pattern that is stamped onto the dough. The embossing is more than mere decoration: It helps the pasta hold the sauce better.

A traditional Ligurian pasta, *trenette* is long and flat, similar to linguine. It is often paired with pesto, and green beans and potatoes are usually cooked in the same water as the pasta. Here, in a twist on the regional classic, yellow beans add an extra hit of color.

TRENETTE WITH PESTO, BEANS & POTATOES

3 cups packed fresh basil leaves

½ cup extra-virgin olive oil

3 tbsp. finely grated Parmigiano-Reggiano

2 tbsp. finely grated Pecorino Romano

2 tbsp. pine nuts

1 clove garlic, finely chopped

Kosher salt and freshly ground black pepper, to taste

1 lb. trenette or linguine

8 oz. green and yellow wax beans, trimmed

8 oz. baby red potatoes, roasted and halved

SERVES 4

1 Purée basil, oil, cheeses, nuts, and garlic in a food processor until smooth. Season with salt and pepper and set aside.

2 In a large pot of generously salted boiling water, cook pasta, stirring occasionally, until half-cooked, about 5 minutes. Add beans and cook, stirring, until pasta is al dente and vegetables are tender, about 3 minutes more. Drain pasta and vegetables, reserving ¼ cup cooking water, and transfer to a large bowl; add pesto and potatoes. Toss to combine, adding a couple tablespoons reserved cooking water, if needed, to make a smooth sauce.

PESTO

Traditional pesto, which originated in Liguria, consists of only basil, garlic, pine nuts, olive oil, salt, and cheese, so the quality and type of each ingredient you use matters. When shopping for basil, look for the youngest, freshest bunch you can find, with an aromatic, rather than a licorice-like, scent. Age is also important when choosing garlic: The younger it is, the sweeter and juicier it will be. Italian-grown pine nuts (*pignoli*) are ideal for their round, rich flavor, but they're expensive. Imported Chinese pine nuts are cheaper and acceptable, although walnuts, soaked in warm water for at least an hour to release any acrid notes, are a better substitute. Use sea salt to heighten the flavors of the other ingredients and to impart a subtle briny flavor. Choose a pale gold olive oil with a delicate, slightly saline flavor. Avoid highly fruity or sharp oils that will overpower the sauce. As for the cheese, Parmigiano-Reggiano is generally preferred for its rich, nutty taste, but Pecorino Romano, a sharp, salty sheep's milk cheese, is also used.

Numerous other pounded herb and vegetable sauces are found around the country. Earthy walnut pesto is a common pasta sauce and bruschetta topping in northern Italy. Parsley pesto with capers and anchovies is a piquant match for rich fish like mackerel, and Sicilian *pesto rosso*, made with almonds and sun-dried tomatoes, is great with linguine or other dried pasta. Pistachio pesto is rather sweet, making it a good choice with roasted vegetables. Peppery arugula pesto is delicious dolloped on ripe tomatoes or on steak, and a touch of ricotta in Calabrese pesto tempers the rich mixture of sweet pepper, eggplant, and tomato.

Orecchiette ("little ears") are a typical pasta of Puglia, where they are often served with greens and meat ragù. Their domed shape is ideal for trapping the tangy goat cheese and chopped bitter greens of this simple-to-assemble dish.

ORECCHIETTE WITH BROCCOLI RABE & GOAT CHEESE

Kosher salt, to taste

1 bunch broccoli rabe (about 1 lb.), coarsely chopped

⅓ cup extra-virgin olive oil

6 cloves garlic, crushed

¾ tsp. chile flakes

12 oz. orecchiette

2 tbsp. grated lemon zest

4 oz. goat cheese, softened

SERVES 2–4

1 In a large pot of generously salted boiling water, cook broccoli rabe until crisp-tender, about 4 minutes. Using a slotted spoon, transfer to a large bowl of ice water. Drain, pat dry, and set aside.

2 Heat oil in a 12" skillet over medium. Add garlic and cook, stirring occasionally, until golden, about 3 minutes. Add chile flakes and cook, stirring frequently, for 30 seconds. Add broccoli rabe, toss, and remove pan from heat; set aside.

3 Meanwhile, bring a pot of generously salted water to a boil. Add pasta and cook until al dente, about 10 minutes. Drain pasta and transfer pasta and lemon zest to reserved skillet over high. Toss to combine with broccoli rabe and season with salt. Divide pasta between bowls and add a dollop of goat cheese to each.

For this sauce from the late Marcella Hazan, the veal is cooked separately and added later to preserve its juiciness. Peel the peppers and the tomatoes so they break down over the heat and form the base of the sauce, as no other liquid is used.

FETTUCCINE WITH VEAL & SWEET PEPPER SAUCE

2   green bell peppers

2   red bell peppers

2   yellow bell peppers

¼   cup extra-virgin olive oil

6   cloves garlic, peeled and crushed

   Kosher salt and freshly ground black pepper, to taste

2   tbsp. canola oil

2   tbsp. butter

½   cup very finely chopped onion

½   lb. ground veal

4   ripe, firm plum tomatoes, peeled and chopped, juice reserved

1   lb. fettuccine

¼   cup grated Grana Padano

SERVES 6

1 Halve each bell pepper lengthwise; stem and seed, then peel with a swivel-blade vegetable peeler. Cut peppers into strips slightly less than 1" wide.

2 Pour olive oil into a 12" skillet. Add garlic, turn heat to medium, and cook, turning garlic as needed, until light brown. Using a slotted spoon, remove garlic from pan and discard. Add bell peppers, salt, and pepper and cook, turning as needed, until tender, about 45 minutes.

3 Meanwhile, heat canola oil and butter in a 10" skillet over medium-high; add onion and cook until golden, 6–8 minutes. Add veal, salt, and pepper and lower heat to medium. Cook, stirring and breaking up meat into small pieces, until browned, 5–7 minutes. Add tomatoes and their juice and simmer for 20 minutes. Add to skillet with peppers and cook 15 minutes more.

4 In a large pot of generously salted boiling water, cook pasta until al dente, 10 minutes; drain. Toss with sauce and Grana Padano. Transfer to a serving platter.

A classic created in the town of Amatrice, in the mountainous area of Lazio, this dish, with its flavorful tomato sauce, has been popular for centuries. Its distinctive ingredients include Pecorino Romano and *guanciale* (cured pork cheek), for which bacon can be substituted.

SPAGHETTI ALL'AMATRICIANA

12 oz. guanciale or thick-cut bacon, cut crosswise into ¼″ strips

2 tbsp. unsalted butter

2 carrots, peeled and finely chopped

1 large yellow onion, finely chopped

Kosher salt, to taste

4 cloves garlic, finely chopped

1 sprig fresh rosemary

1 sprig fresh sage

2 tbsp. red wine

1 28-oz. can whole peeled tomatoes, crushed by hand

2 tbsp. extra-virgin olive oil

2 tsp. freshly ground black pepper

1 tsp. chile flakes

1 lb. spaghetti

Finely grated Pecorino Romano, to garnish

Thinly sliced fresh flat-leaf parsley, to garnish

SERVES 6-8

1 Cook guanciale in a 6-qt. saucepan over medium heat until crisp, about 15 minutes. Using a slotted spoon, transfer guanciale to paper towels to drain; set aside. Add butter, carrots, onion, and salt to pan and cook, stirring, until soft, about 6 minutes. Add half of garlic, the rosemary, and sage and cook, stirring, until fragrant, about 2 minutes. Add wine and cook until evaporated, about 5 minutes. Add tomatoes; reduce heat to medium-low and cook, partially covered and stirring occasionally, until reduced and thickened, about 2 hours. Discard rosemary and sage. Transfer sauce to a blender, purée, and then return to pan. Stir in ¾ of reserved guanciale, the remaining garlic, the oil, pepper, and chile flakes. Set aside and keep warm.

2 Meanwhile, bring a large pot of generously salted water to a boil. Add spaghetti and cook, stirring occasionally, until al dente, about 8 minutes. Drain pasta and add to pan with sauce; toss to coat. Divide pasta and sauce among serving bowls and garnish with remaining guanciale, Pecorino, and parsley.

Shells are the ideal pasta to pair with a light sauce of stock punctuated with mushrooms, peas, and bacon, as their recesses will capture the flavorful ingredients. Orecchiette or farfalle would work well, too.

SHELLS WITH MUSHROOMS, PEAS & BACON

2 tbsp. extra-virgin olive oil

2 tbsp. unsalted butter

4 slices bacon, cut crosswise into ¼" strips

6 oz. portobello mushrooms, cut into 1" pieces

1 small yellow onion, finely chopped

1 cup chicken stock

1 cup fresh or frozen peas

1 lb. medium pasta shells

1 cup grated Parmigiano-Reggiano, plus more for serving

Kosher salt and freshly ground black pepper, to taste

SERVES 6

1 Heat oil and butter in a 12" skillet over medium-high. Add bacon and cook until crisp, 6 minutes. Using a slotted spoon, transfer bacon to paper towels to drain. Add mushrooms and onion and cook until golden, 6–8 minutes. Add stock and peas and cook until reduced by half, 10 minutes. Keep warm.

2 In a large pot of generously salted boiling water, cook pasta until al dente, about 8 minutes. Drain, reserving ¼ cup cooking water; toss pasta and cooking water with warm sauce, bacon, Parmigiano, salt, and pepper. Transfer to a serving platter and garnish with more Parmigiano.

Lamb appears frequently in the cuisine of Abruzzo, where shepherds still practice the thousand-year-old tradition of *transumanza,* the seasonal movement of flocks of sheep from lowlands to mountains and back again. *Spaghetti alla chitarra* are long noodles that are shaped by pressing a sheet of pasta against a frame fitted with metal strings that resemble the strings of a guitar (*chitarra*).

SPAGHETTI ALLA CHITARRA WITH LAMB & SWEET PEPPERS

½ cup extra-virgin olive oil

1 lb. ground lamb

3 bay leaves

3 cloves garlic, thinly sliced

Kosher salt and freshly ground black pepper, to taste

½ cup white wine

1½ cups lamb or chicken stock

1 15-oz. can whole peeled tomatoes, crushed by hand

2 large red bell peppers, stemmed, seeded, and sliced ¼″ thick

1 large yellow bell pepper, stemmed, seeded, and sliced ¼″ thick

1 lb. spaghetti alla chitarra or thick spaghetti

Grated Pecorino Romano, to garnish

SERVES 6-8

1 Heat oil in a 6-qt. saucepan over medium-high. Cook lamb, stirring and breaking up meat into small pieces, until browned, 6–8 minutes. Add bay leaves, garlic, salt, and pepper and cook until garlic is golden, 2–3 minutes. Stir in wine and cook until reduced by half, 2–3 minutes. Add stock, tomatoes, salt, and pepper and bring to a simmer. Reduce heat to medium-low. Cook, stirring occasionally, until sauce is slightly thickened, 35–40 minutes. Stir in bell peppers and cook until peppers are tender but not falling apart, 4–6 minutes. Discard bay leaves.

2 Meanwhile, in a large pot of generously salted boiling water, cook pasta until al dente, 10–12 minutes. Drain pasta and transfer to pan with sauce. Add salt and pepper and, using tongs, toss pasta in sauce. Divide pasta between bowls and garnish with Pecorino.

Southern Italian cooking is noted for its generous use of chile flakes, and this popular seafood pasta is no exception. The spiciness infuses both the rich crab and the lush, slightly creamy sauce that bathes the dish.

SPAGHETTI WITH SPICY CRAB SAUCE

⅓   cup extra-virgin olive oil

1   lb. frozen cooked king crab legs, defrosted and cut into 3″ pieces

1   tsp. celery seed

¾   tsp. chile flakes

8   leaves fresh basil, plus more leaves, torn, to garnish

1   large onion, finely chopped

4   cloves garlic, crushed

2   28-oz. cans whole peeled tomatoes, crushed by hand

2   tbsp. half-and-half

1   lb. lump crabmeat

Kosher salt and freshly ground black pepper, to taste

1   lb. spaghetti

SERVES 4

1 Heat oil in a 6-qt. saucepan over high. Add crab legs and cook, turning occasionally, about 5 minutes; transfer to a plate. Add celery seed, chile flakes, basil, onion, and garlic to pot and cook, stirring occasionally, until onion is soft, about 9 minutes. Transfer mixture to a blender along with tomatoes and half-and-half; purée. Return purée to pot over medium. Add reserved crab pieces and any juices from plate and simmer, stirring occasionally, for 30 minutes. Add crabmeat, salt, and pepper and cook for 15 minutes more. Cover and set aside.

2 In a large pot of generously salted boiling water, cook pasta, stirring occasionally, until al dente, about 8 minutes. Drain pasta, transfer to sauce, and toss to combine. Serve garnished with basil.

In the summer, when both lobsters and herbs are abundant, this dish celebrates the best of sea and garden. Simmering the lobsters in the sauce on a low temperature for a long time extracts the flavor from the shells—just be sure to keep an eye on the skillet so that it doesn't get too hot and you don't overcook the meat.

LINGUINE WITH LOBSTER SAUCE

2	1¼–1½-lb. live lobsters
¼	cup extra-virgin olive oil
	Leaves from ½ bunch fresh flat-leaf parsley, finely chopped
2	cloves garlic, finely chopped
½	green bell pepper, stemmed, seeded, and finely chopped
1½	cups tomato purée
1½	tbsp. tomato paste
1	tbsp. chopped fresh basil
1	tsp. chopped fresh mint
1	tsp. chile flakes
	Kosher salt and freshly ground black pepper, to taste
1	lb. linguine

SERVES 4

1 Plunge a sharp knife into the top of each lobster's head just behind its eyes, then set lobsters aside.

2 Heat oil in a large, deep skillet over medium. Add parsley, garlic, and bell pepper and cook until fragrant, about 2 minutes. Stir in tomato purée, tomato paste, basil, mint, chile flakes, salt, and pepper. Add lobsters, belly sides down and tails flattened out, and reduce heat to medium-low. Cover and simmer, stirring sauce and turning lobsters occasionally, until lobster shells turn bright red and meat is cooked through, about 45 minutes.

3 Remove lobsters from sauce and set aside to cool. When lobsters are cool enough to handle, crack shells with a mallet or handle of a large knife, then remove all meat from shells, working over tomato sauce to catch lobster juices. Discard shells, cut lobster meat into bite-size chunks, and return to sauce.

4 In a large pot of generously salted boiling water, cook linguine until al dente, 9 minutes. Drain pasta, then add to lobster and sauce. Toss and continue to cook for 3–5 minutes before serving.

A delicious marriage of mussels and creamy beans, the sauce for this fragrant dish is traditionally poured over *pasta mista,* a mixture of small and broken pasta shapes. Pasta odds and ends in the pantry? Add them to the pot.

PASTA MISTA WITH BEANS & MUSSELS

Kosher salt and freshly ground black pepper, to taste

7 oz. mixed dried small pasta, such as orzo, and broken linguine and fusilli

1 15-oz. can cannellini beans, drained and rinsed

¾ cup extra-virgin olive oil

4 cloves garlic, thinly sliced

2 ribs celery, finely chopped

½ tsp. chile flakes

1½ lb. mussels, scrubbed and debearded

10 oz. cherry tomatoes, halved

20 fresh basil leaves, torn into pieces

SERVES 4

1 In a large pot of generously salted boiling water, cook pasta until al dente, about 5 minutes. Drain, reserving 1½ cups cooking water; set aside. Add half of beans and 1 cup pasta cooking water to a blender and purée; set aside.

2 Heat ½ cup oil in a 12″ skillet over medium-high. Add garlic, celery, and chile flakes and cook, stirring, until celery is soft, about 8 minutes. Raise heat to high and add remaining pasta cooking water, mussels, and tomatoes. Cook, covered, until mussels open, 2–3 minutes; discard any mussels that failed to open. Uncover and add reserved pasta and both puréed and whole beans; cook, stirring, until warmed through, about 5 minutes more. Stir in remaining oil, the basil, salt, and pepper and serve.

This colorful seafood pasta draws its inspiration from the fishermen's meals that originated on the docks of Italian seaside villages, where the leftovers of the catch—clams, shrimp, squid—were thrown into the pot and served over pasta. In this version, the lobster shells are cooked and puréed along with the aromatics and wine to create the sauce.

BUCATINI AI FRUTTI DI MARE

1	2-lb. live lobster
1	cup extra-virgin olive oil
1	tbsp. chile flakes
6	cloves garlic, chopped
2	carrots, peeled and sliced
1	bulb fennel, trimmed and sliced, fronds reserved to garnish
1	leek, white part only, rinsed and sliced
1	medium yellow onion, sliced
1	cup dry white wine
½	cup fresh carrot juice
1	tbsp. saffron threads
1	tsp. chopped fresh thyme
1½	lb. littleneck or Manila clams, scrubbed
12	raw jumbo shrimp, peeled and deveined, tails on
8	whole cleaned squid and their tentacles, tubes sliced
1	28-oz. can whole peeled tomatoes, crushed by hand
1	lb. bucatini
	Kosher salt, to taste
	Grated zest of 1 lemon

SERVES 4-6

1 Cook lobster in boiling water until tender, 12–15 minutes; let cool. Remove and chop meat; chop shells.

2 Heat ½ cup oil in an 8-qt. saucepan over medium-high; cook chopped lobster shells until golden, 7–8 minutes. Add chile flakes, half of the garlic, the carrots, sliced fennel, the leek, and onion and cook until soft, 8–10 minutes. Add half of the wine and cook until evaporated, 2–3 minutes. Add carrot juice, saffron, thyme, and 1½ cups water and simmer for 10 minutes. Purée in a blender and strain sauce.

3 Wipe pan clean. Heat remaining oil over medium-high. Cook remaining garlic and wine, the clams, shrimp, squid, and tomatoes, covered, until clams open, 5–7 minutes; discard any clams that failed to open.

4 Meanwhile, bring a large pot of generously salted water to a boil. Add pasta and cook, stirring occassionally, until al dente, 10–12 minutes. Drain pasta, transfer to sauce along with reserved lobster meat, salt, and zest and cook for 3 minutes. Garnish with reserved fennel fronds.

Risotto is widely served in northern Italy, where it is often preferred over pasta. Half of the mushrooms in this recipe are folded into the rice, lending it an earthy flavor; the remainder are roasted and used as a crisp, meaty garnish.

MUSHROOM RISOTTO

6	cups chicken stock
8	dried porcini mushrooms
3	tbsp. unsalted butter
1	large yellow onion, finely chopped
2	cups Arborio rice
1	cup white wine
2	lb. mixed fresh mushrooms, such as chanterelles, cremini, hen of the woods, oyster, and porcini, brushed clean and cut or torn into bite-size pieces
1/3	cup extra-virgin olive oil
1	tbsp. coarsely chopped fresh thyme
6	cloves garlic, unpeeled
	Kosher salt and freshly ground black pepper, to taste
8	oz. crème fraîche
1/2	cup grated Parmigiano-Reggiano

SERVES 6

1 Bring stock to a boil in a 2-qt. saucepan over medium and add porcini; cook until soft, 6–8 minutes. Strain, reserving mushrooms, and keep stock warm.

2 Melt butter in a 6-qt. saucepan over medium-high. Cook onion until golden, 6–8 minutes. Add rice and cook until lightly toasted, about 4 minutes. Add wine and cook until evaporated, about 2 minutes. Add 1/2 cup stock and cook, stirring often, until stock is mostly absorbed, 2–3 minutes. Continue adding stock 1/2 cup at a time, stirring until absorbed before adding more, until rice is tender and creamy, about 20 minutes total. Finely chop reserved porcini and add to risotto.

3 Meanwhile, heat oven to 450°F. Toss fresh mushrooms, oil, thyme, garlic, salt, and pepper on a baking sheet and roast until mushrooms are browned and garlic is tender, 10–12 minutes. Peel and mash garlic. Stir half of mushrooms into the risotto, along with the garlic, crème fraîche, Parmigiano, salt, and pepper. Garnish with remaining mushrooms.

A finishing touch of tart lemon zest and fragrant rosemary brightens a creamy risotto from Piedmont. The French, who ruled this northern Italian region at various times, left a definitive mark on the cuisine with the wide use of butter and cheese.

LEMON-ROSEMARY RISOTTO

1 cup grated Parmigiano-Reggiano

1 tbsp. finely chopped fresh rosemary

Grated zest of 3 lemons, plus 1 tbsp. lemon juice

6 cups chicken stock

3 tbsp. extra-virgin olive oil

4 cloves garlic, finely chopped

1 small yellow onion, finely chopped

2 cups Arborio rice

⅓ cup white wine

3 tbsp. unsalted butter

Kosher salt and freshly ground black pepper, to taste

SERVES 6

1 Combine Parmigiano, rosemary, and zest in a bowl; set aside. Bring stock to a simmer in a 2-qt. saucepan over medium and keep warm.

2 Heat oil in a 6-qt. saucepan over medium-high and cook garlic and onion until soft, 5–7 minutes. Add rice and cook until opaque, 3–4 minutes. Add wine and cook until absorbed, 1–2 minutes. Add ½ cup stock and cook, stirring often, until stock is mostly absorbed, 2–3 minutes. Add another ½ cup stock and repeat process until all of stock is used, about 20 minutes. Continue cooking until rice is al dente, 2–3 minutes. Remove from heat and stir in half of Parmigiano mixture, the butter, salt, and pepper. Garnish with remaining Parmigiano mixture.

Clam juice amplifies the brininess of this seafood risotto, which relies on such sharp flavors as lime juice and cayenne to enhance the taste of the shrimp and clams.

CLAM RISOTTO WITH GRILLED SHRIMP

5   cups fish stock

3   tbsp. unsalted butter

0   cloves garlic, finely chopped

1   small shallot, finely chopped

1   cup Arborio rice

¼   cup white wine

1½   cups packed fresh baby spinach

⅓   cup clam juice

¼   cup grated Parmigiano-Reggiano

¼   cup heavy cream

20   hard-shell clams, such as littleneck or Manila, scrubbed

Kosher salt and freshly ground black pepper, to taste

16   jumbo shrimp, peeled and deveined, tails on

1½   tsp. paprika

¼   tsp. cayenne pepper

Lime wedges, for serving

SERVES 4

1 Bring stock to a simmer in a 2-qt. saucepan over medium and keep warm. Melt butter in a 6-qt. saucepan over medium-high. Add garlic and shallot and cook until soft, 3–4 minutes. Add rice and cook until lightly toasted, about 4 minutes. Stir in wine and cook until evaporated, 1–2 minutes. Add ½ cup stock and cook, stirring often, until stock is mostly absorbed, 2–3 minutes. Continue adding stock ½ cup at a time, stirring until absorbed before adding more, until rice is tender and creamy, about 20 minutes total. Stir in spinach, clam juice, Parmigiano, cream, clams, salt, and pepper. Cook, covered, until clams open, 5–7 minutes; discard any clams that failed to open.

2 Build a medium-hot fire in a charcoal grill, or heat a gas grill to medium-high. (Alternatively, heat a cast-iron grill pan over medium-high.) Season shrimp with paprika, cayenne, and salt and grill, flipping once, until slightly charred and cooked, 3–5 minutes. Divide risotto between 4 plates, top with shrimp, and serve with lime wedges.

A specialty of Naples, this turnover (the name of which translates to "big socks") is essentially an enclosed pizza. Neapolitan pizza is often eaten at the table with a knife and fork; a calzone, in contrast, can be eaten on the run.

CALZONE WITH ANCHOVIES, TOMATOES & MOZZARELLA

FOR THE DOUGH

1	¼-oz. package active dry yeast
¼	cup water, heated to 115°F
1½	cups all-purpose flour, plus more for dusting
1½	cups cake flour
1	tsp. salt
	Extra-virgin olive oil, for coating and brushing
¼	cup cornmeal

FOR THE FILLING

½	lb. fresh mozzarella, sliced into 8 pieces
16	anchovies, drained
1	14-oz. can whole peeled tomatoes, drained and chopped
2	tsp. finely chopped fresh oregano leaves

MAKES 4

1 Make the dough: Dissolve yeast in water in a large bowl and let sit until foamy, about 10 minutes. Combine flours and salt in a bowl. Add 1 cup flour mixture to yeast and stir with a wooden spoon. Add ½ cup water, then 1 cup flour mixture. Mix well, then work in remaining 1 cup flour mixture. Gradually add another ¼ cup water to make a soft, moist dough. Turn out dough onto a lightly floured surface and knead until smooth, 10–12 minutes. Divide dough into 4 balls. Lightly coat the inside of 4 small bowls with oil. Place 1 ball of dough in each bowl. Cover with damp cloths and set in a warm spot to rise until doubled in size, 1½–2 hours.

2 Place a pizza stone in oven and heat to 450°F. On a floured surface, stretch 1 ball of dough into a thin 9″ round. Place 2 slices mozzarella, 4 anchovies, and 2–3 tbsp. tomatoes on one side of 1 round of dough. Sprinkle with oregano, fold dough over, and pinch to seal. Repeat process with remaining dough. Sprinkle cornmeal on pizza stone, place calzones on top, and brush with a little oil. Bake until golden, about 15 minutes.

In Rome, *pizza rustica* is often an on-the-go snack sold wrapped in wax paper. When this version, covered with thinly sliced potatoes, yellow onion, and rosemary, is baked, magic happens: The crust gets perfectly crispy, the potatoes and onions become golden brown, and the rosemary gives off an enticing fragrance.

POTATO & ROSEMARY PIZZA RUSTICA

1   recipe Basic Pizza Dough (page 121)

FOR THE TOPPING

6   Yukon gold potatoes

½   tsp. kosher salt, plus more to taste

½   yellow onion, cut into ½" pieces

¾   cup extra-virgin olive oil
    Flour, for dusting

2   tbsp. fresh rosemary leaves

MAKES 2

1 Make the dough, dividing it into 2 balls rather than 4.

2 Make the topping: Peel and very thinly slice potatoes on a mandoline or with a very sharp knife, transferring them to a large bowl of ice water as sliced. Soak potatoes for 30 minutes to remove excess starch, then drain in a colander. Repeat soaking and draining process 2 more times. Set colander with potatoes over a large bowl. Toss potatoes with ½ tsp. salt and set aside to drain for 10 minutes. Transfer potatoes to a medium bowl. Add onion and 1 tbsp. oil, toss well, and set aside.

3 Heat oven to 475°F. Grease 2 baking sheets with 2 tbsp. oil each and set aside. Transfer dough to a lightly floured surface and shape each ball into a rectangle.

Transfer each piece of dough onto a prepared baking sheet. Using your hands, gently flatten and spread dough out to edges of pan in a very thin rectangle. (Dough will shrink back a bit each time you spread it out, so let it rest for 10–15 minutes each time.) Brush each dough slab with 2 tbsp. oil. Evenly spread half the potato mixture over surface of each slab, leaving a 1" border around edges. Season to taste with salt, drizzle remaining oil over each, and sprinkle each with 1 tbsp. rosemary.

4 Bake until crust is crisp and dark golden brown around the edges and potatoes are ringed golden brown, about 20 minutes, rotating pans halfway through baking. Transfer pizzas to a cutting board and serve hot or at room temperature.

PIZZA PRIMER

Being able to turn out perfect pizza dough is a basic skill that every good Italian cook masters. This dough is quick to make and is versatile enough to hold heavy layers of sauce and cheese or a light sprinkle of parmesan and fresh herbs.

BASIC PIZZA DOUGH

1	cup water, heated to 115°F
1	tsp. honey
1	¼-oz. package active dry yeast
¾	cup warm beer
2	tbsp. extra-virgin olive oil, plus more for serving
3	cups bread flour, plus more for dusting
1	tsp. kosher salt, plus more to taste

MAKES DOUGH FOR FOUR 10" THIN-CRUST PIZZAS

1 In a large bowl, stir together water, honey, and yeast and let sit until foamy, about 10 minutes. Add beer and oil and stir until smooth. Add flour and salt and stir until a rough dough forms. Transfer to a lightly floured surface and knead until smooth, about 8 minutes. Cover with a towel and let rise in a warm spot until doubled in size, about 45 minutes.

2 Divide dough into 4 balls and cover with a towel; let sit in a warm spot for another 30 minutes. Proceed as directed in individual pizza recipes.

TIPS When the dough is ready to shape into balls, it should be soft and slightly sticky but not stick to your hands. If it seems too sticky, add a little more flour.

If the warm spot you have chosen to leave the dough to rise is outdoors, dampen the towel before covering the dough. This will help keep the dough from drying out on the top.

The dough can be made ahead, shaped into balls, and frozen for up to 3 months. When you are ready to use it, bring it to room temperature and let it rise for 30 minutes as directed in step 2.

TOPPINGS A nearly unlimited number of ingredients taste delicious atop a freshly baked pizza. Here are some outstanding combinations to try on your next pie.

PUTTANESCA anchovies + capers + pitted black olives + crushed red chile flakes + finely chopped garlic

SICILIAN-STYLE ALLA NORMA thinly sliced eggplant + ricotta + fresh basil leaves

CARNE hot Italian sausage (casings removed) + sliced pepperoni + cubed salami + prosciutto

CARBONARA cubed guanciale or pancetta + shredded pecorino + black pepper + an egg

POTATO & ANCHOVY paper-thin potato slices + basil pesto + anchovies

CRISPY KALE & MUSHROOM smoked mozzarella + sliced porcini mushrooms + stemmed and chopped cavolo nero kale massaged with extra-virgin olive oil

FOUR CHEESE fresh mozzarella + ricotta + grated Parmigiano-Reggiano + goat cheese + thinly sliced garlic + fresh rosemary

The cultivation of arugula dates to Roman times, and in Italy, this aromatic green is liberally added to many dishes beyond salad. Here, it provides a peppery kick to a meat-laden pizza. Drizzle the pizza with olive oil before serving for another layer of flavor.

PIZZA WITH SAUSAGE, ONION & ARUGULA

1   recipe Basic Pizza Dough (page 121)

FOR THE TOPPING

1   28-oz. can whole peeled tomatoes, crushed by hand

Kosher salt and freshly ground black pepper, to taste

1   lb. hot Italian sausage, casings removed

Fine semolina, for dusting

1   lb. fresh mozzarella, sliced

1   red onion, thinly sliced

2   cups baby arugula

Extra-virgin olive oil, for drizzling

MAKES 4

1 Make the dough.

2 Make the topping: Season tomatoes with salt and pepper and set aside.

3 Heat a 10″ skillet over medium-high. Add sausage and cook, breaking up meat into small pieces, until browned, 7–8 minutes; set aside.

4 Place a pizza stone in oven and heat to 425°F. Working in 4 batches, dust 1 ball dough with semolina. Using your fingertips, press dough into a 10″ round about ¼″ thick. Hold dough straight up, and with fingertips circling crust, slide fingers around crust in a circular motion as you would turn a steering wheel, until dough in center is stretched to about ⅛″ thick; transfer to a semolina-dusted pizza peel. Leaving a 1″ border around the edge, top with ¼ each of tomato sauce, sausage, mozzarella, and onion. Slide pizza onto stone and bake until cheese melts and crust is puffed and charred in spots, 10–12 minutes. Transfer to a cutting board and season with salt and pepper; top with arugula and drizzle with oil. Serve hot.

This sweet-smoky pizza is adapted from one made by Antonio Starita, owner of the renowned Pizzeria Starita in Naples. He once famously served his version of the pie to Pope John Paul II—hence its nickname, *pizza del papa,* or "the Pope's pizza."

PIZZA WITH BUTTERNUT SQUASH & SMOKED MOZZARELLA

1   recipe Basic Pizza Dough (page 121)

FOR THE TOPPING

1   small butternut squash (about 1 lb.), peeled, seeded, and cut into 1″ pieces

¾   cup extra-virgin olive oil, plus more for drizzling

    Kosher salt, to taste

1¼ lb. smoked mozzarella, thinly sliced

2   tbsp. heavy cream

2   tbsp. ricotta

1   tsp. chile flakes

2   small zucchini, thinly sliced

1   red bell pepper, stemmed, seeded, and cut into 1″ pieces

1   yellow bell pepper, stemmed, seeded, and cut into 1″ pieces

    Fine semolina, for dusting

16 fresh basil leaves

MAKES 4

1 Make the dough.

2 Make the topping: Heat oven to 500°F. Toss butternut squash with ¼ cup oil and salt on a baking sheet and bake until tender, 20–25 minutes. Transfer to a food processor with ¼ lb. mozzarella, cream, ricotta, and salt and purée until smooth.

3 Heat ¼ cup oil and chile flakes in a 12″ skillet over medium-high. Add zucchini and salt and cook until golden, 8–10 minutes; transfer to a bowl. Add remaining oil to skillet and return to medium-high. Add bell peppers and cook until tender, 5–7 minutes.

4 Heat broiler, place a pizza stone 4″ under it, and heat for 30 minutes. Working in 4 batches, dust 1 ball dough with semolina. Using your fingertips, press dough into a 10″ round about ¼″ thick. Hold dough straight up, and with fingertips circling crust, slide fingers around crust in a circular motion as you would turn a steering wheel, until dough in center is stretched to about ⅛″ thick; transfer to a semolina-dusted pizza peel. Leaving a 1″ border around edge, spread ½ cup squash purée over dough and distribute ¼ each of zucchini, peppers, remaining mozzarella, and the basil leaves; drizzle with oil. Slide pizza onto stone and broil until cheese melts and crust is puffed and charred in spots, 3–4 minutes. Transfer to a cutting board and serve hot.

There are several layers of different yet complementary onion flavors in this vegetarian pie. A purée of sautéed white onions forms the base, which is topped with curls of shallots, red onions, and leeks, which are then sprinkled with fresh scallions and chives.

SIX-ONION PIZZA

1   recipe Basic Pizza Dough
    (page 121)

FOR THE TOPPING

5   tbsp. extra-virgin olive oil

    Leaves from 12 sprigs
    fresh thyme

2   large white onions, thinly
    sliced lengthwise

1   bay leaf

    Kosher salt and freshly
    ground black pepper,
    to taste

8   oz. leeks, white part only,
    halved lengthwise, rinsed,
    and cut into ¼"-thick slices

8   oz. red onions, thinly
    sliced lengthwise

8   oz. shallots, thinly sliced
    lengthwise

    Flour, for dusting

2   cups finely grated
    Grana Padano

4   scallions, trimmed and
    thinly sliced

1   bunch fresh chives,
    thinly sliced

MAKES 4

1 Make the dough.

2 Make the topping: Combine 2 tbsp. oil, thyme, white onions, bay leaf, salt, and pepper in a 12" skillet over medium-low. Cook, stirring occasionally, until onions are very soft but not browned, about 30 minutes. Remove and discard bay leaf. Transfer onions to a food processor or blender and purée until smooth; set aside.

3 Return skillet to medium and add 1 tbsp. oil. Add leeks, season with salt and pepper, and cook, stirring occasionally, until very soft but not browned, about 15 minutes. Transfer to a bowl and set aside. Heat remaining oil in skillet, add red onions and shallots, and season with salt and pepper. Cook, stirring occasionally, until very tender and lightly browned, about 18 minutes. Transfer to bowl with leeks and stir to combine.

4 Heat oven to 500°F. Working in 4 batches, place 1 ball dough on a lightly floured work surface.Using your fingertips, press dough into a 10" round about ¼" thick. Hold dough straight up, and with fingertips circling crust, slide fingers around rust in a circular motion as you would turn a steering wheel, until dough in center is stretched to about ⅛" thick. Place dough round on a parchment paper–lined baking sheet and, working quickly, spread about 2 tbsp. onion purée over dough, leaving a 1" border around edge; sprinkle evenly with about ¼ cup leek mixture. Sprinkle ½ cup Grana Padano over leek mixture and transfer to oven. Bake until browned and crisp at the edges, about 12 minutes. Sprinkle each pizza with ¼ each of scallions and chives before serving.

FISH
&MEAT

Adapted from Lidia Bastianich's *Lidia's Italy,* this dish hails from Italy's Adriatic coast and borrows its name from the neighbors across the sea: *Buzara* is Croatian for "stew." Tomato paste, white wine, and plenty of fresh parsley make for a simple yet delectable broth—you'll want some crusty bread to sop it up.

SHRIMP BUZARA-STYLE

¼ cup extra-virgin olive oil

3 cloves garlic, finely chopped

2 shallots, finely chopped

1½ tbsp. tomato paste

1 cup white wine

24 large shell-on shrimp (about 1 lb.), deveined

Kosher salt and freshly ground black pepper, to taste

2 tbsp. finely chopped fresh flat-leaf parsley

SERVES 4

Heat oil in a 12″ skillet over medium-high. Add garlic and shallots and cook for 1–2 minutes. Add tomato paste and cook 2 minutes more. Add wine and ½ cup water; reduce for 6 minutes. Add shrimp, salt, and pepper and cook, flipping shrimp halfway, 3–4 minutes, or until shrimp are pink and cooked through. Transfer to a serving platter and sprinkle with parsley.

Resting on a bed of couscous-like Sardinian pasta called fregola, the grouper here is spicy—Italian-American chef Mario Carbone uses Calabrian chiles to add punch. He steams the fish instead of searing it, taking inspiration from chefs in Hong Kong, where he recently opened a restaurant.

STEAMED GROUPER IN CHILE OIL

1¼ cups extra-virgin olive oil

2 tbsp. dried whole Calabrian chiles, plus ⅓ cup crushed chiles

3 sprigs fresh thyme

2 cloves garlic, thinly sliced

1 sprig fresh rosemary

Kosher salt and freshly ground black pepper, to taste

6 oz. fresh garlic chives or scallions, trimmed and cut into 2" pieces

3 ribs celery, thinly sliced on the bias, plus ½ cup inner celery leaves

2 bulbs fennel, trimmed, halved, and thinly sliced

3 cups fregola

½ cup packed fresh curly parsley leaves (half coarsely chopped)

½ cup packed fresh mint leaves (half coarsely chopped)

6 5-oz. boneless, skin-on red grouper fillets

SERVES 6

1 Bring 1 cup oil, whole chiles, thyme, garlic, and rosemary to a simmer in a 1-qt. saucepan over medium; cook for 1 minute and remove from heat. Stir in crushed chiles. Let oil steep for 3 hours at room temperature or transfer oil to an airtight container and chill overnight. Let chilled oil come to room temperature before using.

2 In a large pot of generously salted boiling water, cook 4 oz. garlic chives, the celery, and fennel until crisp-tender, 30–60 seconds. Using a slotted spoon, transfer vegetables to an ice bath until chilled; drain and set aside. Add fregola to pot of water and cook until al dente, about 20 minutes; drain and transfer to a serving bowl. Stir in remaining oil and the chopped parsley and mint; season with salt and pepper. Sprinkle cooked garlic chives, celery, and fennel, and parsley and mint leaves over top. Cover with plastic wrap and keep warm.

3 Bring 1" water to a boil in a 14" wok fitted with a two-tiered 11" bamboo steamer. Divide grouper fillets between 2 pie plates and season with salt and pepper; place in steamer and cover. Steam until fillets are cooked through, about 8 minutes. To serve, spoon reserved fregola into shallow bowls and top with fillets, skin side up. Spoon chile oil over fish and garnish with remaining garlic chives.

ABOUT FREGOLA

This pellet-shaped pasta comes from the island of Sardinia, off the west coast of Italy. Fregola, or fregula, is made from semolina dough that has been rolled into tiny balls and toasted in the oven. It has a subtle nuttiness and a texture similar to that of Israeli couscous.

Calabria has a long tradition of preserving foods, so it comes as no surprise that salty, briny olives and capers are hallmarks of the region's cooking. Here, the two are used in a vibrant sauce spooned over meaty swordfish.

SWORDFISH STEAKS WITH OLIVES & CAPERS

4   swordfish steaks (about 6 oz. each and ½″ thick)

Kosher salt and freshly ground black pepper, to taste

¼   cup extra-virgin olive oil

3   cloves garlic, finely chopped

¾   cup large green olives, pitted and coarsely chopped

½   cup white wine

¼   cup capers, drained and rinsed

1   tbsp. fresh lemon juice, plus lemon wedges for serving

½   cup celery leaves, to garnish

SERVES 4

1 Season swordfish with salt and pepper. Heat oil in a 12″ skillet over high. Working in 2 batches, cook swordfish, flipping once, until brown on outside and medium-rare inside, about 3 minutes. Transfer fish to a serving platter and keep warm.

2 Return skillet to medium. Add garlic and cook until soft, about 2 minutes. Add olives, wine, and capers; cook until almost all the liquid evaporates, about 8 minutes. Add lemon juice and spoon sauce over fish. Garnish with celery leaves and serve with lemon wedges.

Mackerel, favored for its distinctive rich, savory flavor, is paired here with lemony fennel and tomatoes that have softened from baking. Make sure the fish skin is completely dry before searing so it can get extra crispy, and serve the fish skin side up so the skin doesn't get soggy on the platter.

MACKEREL WITH LEMON & FENNEL

4	oz. country-style bread, torn into ½" pieces
½	cup plus 2 tbsp. extra-virgin olive oil
6	cloves garlic, thinly sliced
1	bulb fennel, trimmed and coarsely chopped, fronds reserved to garnish
1	pint cherry tomatoes
	Kosher salt and freshly ground black pepper, to taste
2	tbsp. fresh lemon juice
4	skin-on mackerel fillets (about 5 oz. each)

1 Heat oven to 375°F. Toss bread, ¼ cup oil, the garlic, fennel, tomatoes, salt, and pepper on a baking sheet and bake until bread is golden, 15–20 minutes. Toss with lemon juice and keep warm.

2 Meanwhile, season fish with salt and pepper. Heat ¼ cup oil in a 12" skillet over medium-high. Cook fish, skin side down, until crispy, about 4 minutes. Flip and cook 1 minute more. Transfer fish to a serving platter and top with reserved bread mixture. Garnish with reserved fennel fronds and drizzle with remaining oil.

SERVES 4

COOKING WHOLE FISH

Cooking a whole fish can be a bit daunting, but once you've done it, it will be easy the next time. Select a fish with clear, bright eyes and shiny, moist skin, planning on about 1 lb. per person, and ask the fishmonger to clean it.

ROASTING Stuff the cavity with aromatics such as dill, parsley, lemon and onion slices, and/or garlic. Before cooking, drizzle the fish with extra-virgin olive oil and season with sea salt and freshly ground black pepper. Place on an oiled baking sheet and bake in a preheated 350°F oven for 10 minutes per inch, or until the flesh bounces back when pressed.

To serve, make a cut with a sharp knife along the backbone from head to tail. Make a crosscut behind the head and another behind the tail. With the flat of the knife parallel to the bone, lift away the flesh. Then, lift the tail to remove the backbone and head with one motion, leaving the other side of the fish neatly filleted.

GRILLING Sardines, trout, sea bass, rock cod, and other fish weighing between 1 and 2 lb. are ideal for grilling. Stuff the cavity as directed for roasting fish, cut 3 or 4 slashes into the flesh on both sides, and then oil the fish well on both sides.

Build a hot fire in the grill and generously oil the grate to prevent sticking. Place the fish on the grate with the tail end farthest from the heat (it cooks more quickly). When the cavity and tail edges begin to crisp (after 8 to 10 minutes for a fish 2" thick), gently lift the fish with a spatula (if the skin does not stick, the fish is ready to flip) and turn it over. Cook until an instant-read thermometer inserted into the thickest part away from bone registers 135°, 8 to 10 minutes longer. Carve as directed above.

This dish from a well-known Venetian fishmonger combines iconic Italian ingredients—garlic, basil, wine, and cheese. Whole shrimp are butterflied and stuffed with Parmigiano-Reggiano and bread crumbs before being drizzled with wine and crisped under the broiler.

VENETIAN-STYLE GRATINÉED SHRIMP

24 large shell-on shrimp, legs removed

6 slices stale white bread, crusts removed

¼ cup finely chopped fresh basil

1 tbsp. grated Parmigiano-Reggiano

1 clove garlic, finely chopped

3 tbsp. extra-virgin olive oil, plus more for serving

Kosher salt and freshly ground black pepper, to taste

½ cup tocai friulano or other dry Friuli white wine

SERVES 4

1 Heat oven to 400°F. To butterfly shrimp, make a deep incision with the tip of a sharp knife in the back just below the head and slice down to the tail, cutting through the shell and about halfway through the meat. Split open shrimp and flatten slightly with your fingertips; set aside.

2 Tear bread into pieces and pulse to coarse crumbs in a food processor. Transfer to a bowl and add basil, Parmigiano, and garlic. Add oil, salt, and pepper, and toss. Stuff each shrimp with some bread-crumb mixture and arrange on a baking sheet. Moisten each shrimp with about 1 tsp. wine and bake for 10 minutes. Turn oven to broil and place baking sheet under broiler. Broil until bread-crumb mixture is lightly charred, about 2 minutes. Drizzle with more oil before serving.

The key to this dish is the flavorful sauce made from the fish scraps. The head and bones are roasted with wine and aromatics before the liquid is strained and emulsified into a concentrated accompaniment to the meaty fish. The mushrooms add an enticing earthy element.

SAUTÉED SEA BASS WITH CHANTERELLES

Canola oil, for frying

8 sprigs fresh flat-leaf parsley

1 2½–3-lb. whole striped sea bass, cleaned and filleted, head and bones reserved

8 tbsp. extra-virgin olive oil

6 bay leaves

1 carrot, peeled and chopped

1 rib celery, chopped

1 yellow onion, chopped

1 cup chardonnay or other white wine

1 tbsp. tomato paste

1 tbsp. flour

Kosher salt and freshly ground black pepper, to taste

6 oz. chanterelles, quartered

SERVES 4

1 Heat oven to 350°F. Heat 2″ canola oil in a 4-qt. saucepan until a deep-fry thermometer reads 325°F. Pick leaves from 2 sprigs parsley and fry in oil until crisp, about 30 seconds. Using a slotted spoon, transfer to paper towels to drain.

2 Cut fish fillets in half crosswise with a sharp knife, then score skin in a crosshatch pattern and set aside. Chop fish head and bones into large pieces and set aside.

3 Heat 2 tbsp. olive oil in a heavy-bottomed medium roasting pan on top of stove over medium-high. Add remaining parsley, the bay leaves, carrot, celery, and onion and cook, stirring often, until just softened, 3–5 minutes. Add fish head and bones; cook, stirring often, until bones begin to turn golden brown, 3–4 minutes. Add wine and tomato paste and cook, stirring and scraping up browned bits on bottom of pan, until alcohol evaporates, about 2 minutes. Whisk flour and 2 cups water together in a bowl until smooth, then stir into pan and bring to a boil. Transfer pan to oven and roast

until liquid has reduced by about half, 25–30 minutes. Strain liquid, discarding solids. Reserve ¼ cup liquid and put remaining liquid into a blender. With motor running, gradually add 2 tbsp. olive oil until sauce is emulsified; season with salt and pepper. Transfer sauce to a small saucepan and keep warm.

4 Heat 1 tbsp. olive oil in a 10″ skillet over medium. Add chanterelles and cook, stirring occasionally, until browned, 3–5 minutes. Add reserved ¼ cup liquid and season with salt and pepper. Remove skillet from heat, cover, and set aside.

5 Heat 2 tbsp. olive oil in a 12″ skillet over high. Season fish fillets with salt and pepper; cook, skin side down, until golden and crisp, 1–1½ minutes. Turn fillets, reduce heat to medium, and cook until fish is just cooked through, 2–5 minutes. To serve, divide fish between plates, skin side up. Top with chanterelles, then spoon sauce over. Drizzle each plate with remaining olive oil and garnish with fried parsley.

At the Dalla Rosa Alda trattoria in Valpolicella, where this beef dish is a specialty, a platter of polenta rests by the wood fire in the kitchen. As orders come in, a slice of polenta is cut off, grilled over the fire, and served alongside the beef. The wine used in the braising liquid, amarone, lends a note of dark dried fruit to the stew.

BEEF BRAISED IN AMARONE

1   750-ml bottle young
     amarone wine

3   cloves garlic, chopped

2   carrots, peeled and
     finely diced

2   ribs celery, finely diced

2   yellow onions, finely diced

1   celery root, peeled and
     finely diced

1   sprig each fresh rosemary,
     thyme, and sage and 2 bay
     leaves, tied together with
     butcher's twine

     Finely grated zest of 1 lemon

1   4-lb. boneless cross-rib
     pot roast

     Kosher salt and freshly
     ground black pepper,
     to taste

3   cups vegetable or meat stock

¾   cup extra-virgin olive oil

     Polenta, for serving

SERVES 6–8

1 Reserve ¼ cup wine and pour remaining wine into a 6-qt. saucepan. Add garlic, carrots, celery, onions, celery root, bundle of herbs, and lemon zest. Season pot roast with salt and pepper and add to pot. Add stock and ¼ cup oil and bring to a simmer over medium-high, skimming any foam that rises to surface. Reduce heat to medium-low, cover, and braise meat, turning every hour, until very tender, about 4 hours. Transfer meat to a cutting board and cover loosely with foil. Remove and discard bundle of herbs from pot. Strain braising broth into a bowl, setting broth and strained vegetable mixture aside separately.

2 Heat ¼ cup oil in a large skillet over medium-high. Add 3 cups vegetable mixture and ½ cup broth (save remaining vegetable mixture and broth for another use), mash to a paste with a potato masher, and cook until liquid evaporates, 6–8 minutes. Add reserved wine and cook, stirring, until wine evaporates, 1–2 minutes. Add remaining oil and cook until sauce darkens and begins to fry, 5–6 minutes. Season with salt and pepper. Slice meat and serve with polenta alongside, spooning sauce on top.

There are a lot of ingredients in traditional meatballs—several meats, herbs, a variety of spices, milk, cheese, and more—but the results are a study in perfect balance. Moist, salty, and airy, with a tiny bit of heat from chile flakes, these meatballs epitomize Italian comfort food.

CLASSIC MEATBALLS

10	oz. ground beef chuck or veal
10	oz. ground pork shoulder
2	oz. finely chopped pork fat or unsmoked bacon
2	oz. prosciutto, finely chopped
1¼	cups loosely packed fresh flat-leaf parsley leaves, finely chopped, plus more to garnish
2	tsp. dried oregano
1½	tsp. fennel seeds
1	tsp. chile flakes
½	tsp. ground cumin
¼	tsp. ground allspice
7	slices white bread, finely ground in a food processor
	Kosher salt and freshly ground black pepper, to taste
⅔	cup ricotta, drained in a sieve for 2 hours
2	tbsp. milk
3	eggs, lightly beaten
6	tbsp. extra-virgin olive oil, plus more for greasing
¼	cup red wine
4	cups canned tomato purée
1	cup beef or veal stock
	Grated Parmigiano-Reggiano, to garnish

SERVES 4-6

1 In a large bowl, combine beef, pork, pork fat, prosciutto, parsley, oregano, fennel seeds, chile flakes, cumin, allspice, and bread crumbs and season generously with salt and pepper. Using your fingers, mix ingredients until combined and set aside. In a bowl, whisk together ricotta, milk, and eggs; add to meat mixture and gently mix until incorporated. Chill for 1 hour.

2 Heat oven to 300°F. Grease 2 rimmed baking sheets with oil and set aside. Using a 2-oz. ice cream scoop, portion mixture, roll into meatballs with your hands, and transfer to greased baking sheets. Heat 3 tbsp. oil in a 3-qt. high-sided skillet over medium-high. Add half the meatballs; cook, turning occasionally, until browned, about 10 minutes. Transfer meatballs to a plate and wipe out skillet. Repeat with remaining oil and meatballs. Return reserved meatballs to skillet along with any juices from the plate. Add wine, increase heat to high, and cook for 2 minutes. Stir in tomato purée and stock, bring to a boil, and tightly cover skillet. Transfer to oven and bake until meatballs are tender and have absorbed some sauce, about 1½ hours. To serve, transfer meatballs to a platter and spoon sauce over. Sprinkle with Parmigiano and parsley.

This simple but delicious recipe is for steak as it is cooked in Florence: on the grill, minimally seasoned, and served rare. Using rosemary sprigs to baste the meat imparts a subtle but lovely herbal note.

BISTECCA ALLA FIORENTINA

2   1½"-thick bone-in porterhouse steaks (about 3½ lb. total weight)

¼   cup extra-virgin olive oil

Kosher salt and freshly ground black pepper, to taste

2   sprigs fresh rosemary

Lemon wedges, for serving

SERVES 4

Build a hot fire in a charcoal grill, or heat a gas grill to high; bank coals or turn off burner on one side. Brush steaks with half of oil and season with salt and pepper. Grill on hottest part of grill, flipping once, until browned, 4–6 minutes. Using rosemary sprigs as a brush, baste steaks with remaining oil. Cook to desired doneness, 4–6 minutes more for medium-rare, or until an instant-read thermometer inserted into meat reads 125°F. If the outside starts to burn before steak is fully cooked, move to cooler side of grill until done. Let steaks rest 10 minutes then slice against grain along bone. Serve with lemon wedges.

Braised veal shanks are a Milanese specialty. Here they are accented with a sweet and tangy pan sauce made with blood oranges and sherry vinegar, which thickens to almost a glaze and burnishes the shanks mahogany. The rich, fall-off-the-bone meat and the unctuous bone marrow at the heart of each shank bone make this dish sublime.

OSSO BUCO WITH BLOOD ORANGE & FENNEL

4   1-lb. pieces veal shank, about 2″ thick

Kosher salt and freshly ground black pepper, to taste

½   cup flour

¼   cup extra-virgin olive oil

½   cup sherry vinegar

3   cups veal stock

2   bulbs fennel, trimmed

2   carrots, peeled and thinly sliced

2   cups fresh blood orange juice

1   blood orange, peeled, seeded, and supremed (page 67)

4   sprigs fresh flat-leaf parsley, to garnish

SERVES 4

1 Heat oven to 325°F. Season shanks with salt and pepper. Place flour on a plate. Dredge shanks in flour, coating well. Heat oil in a large ovenproof skillet over medium-high. Add shanks and brown on all sides, 10–15 minutes. Remove shanks and set aside. Deglaze skillet with vinegar, stirring and scraping up browned bits from bottom of pan. Reduce vinegar by half, until slightly syrupy, 3–5 minutes; add stock. Return shanks to skillet, cover, and braise in oven for 45 minutes. Turn shanks and continue cooking for another 45 minutes.

2 Split fennel from top to bottom, then cut lengthwise into ½″-thick slices. Add fennel, carrots, and orange juice to shanks and continue to cook, covered, until vegetables are tender, about 45 minutes.

3 Using a slotted spoon, transfer shanks and vegetables to a serving platter. Simmer sauce, skimming occasionally, over medium-high for 4–5 minutes. Stir in orange segments. Ladle sauce over shanks and vegetables and serve garnished with parsley.

ITALIAN HERBS

Herbs are essential to Italian cooking, their aroma and taste bringing added depth of flavor and earthiness to most dishes. Use them fresh in salads, cook them down in sauces, or add them to dressings and marinades. Here are the most commonly used varieties.

SWEET BASIL Sweet basil has a complex aroma with notes of anise and clove. It is the base of Liguria's famed *pesto genovese* and pairs perfectly with tomatoes. Basil bruises easily, turning black, but retains its flavor.

ITALIAN FLAT-LEAF PARSLEY Tangy and herbaceous, flat-leaf parsley, which has a more persistent flavor than its curly kin, can be used in salads, such as the Octopus & Potato Salad on page 61, or added to cooked dishes at the last minute, such as Chicken Cacciatore on page 148, where it delivers a light, peppery finish.

MARJORAM & OREGANO Often confused for each other, marjoram and oregano are similar in look and taste, but oregano has a slightly more robust flavor, with notes of lemon, and marjoram is a touch sweeter. Oregano is commonly used in pasta and pizza sauces. Marjoram, with its more delicate profile, is best added to cooked dishes at the last moment, so the heat doesn't diminish its flavor.

ROSEMARY Rosemary leaves can be rather tough, so be sure to chop them finely before using. Slightly bitter, with notes of pine, rosemary has a strong flavor that holds up during long cooking.

SAGE Sage has an assertive flavor with a warm spiciness and is thought to aid in the digestion of fatty and oily foods. It complements a wide variety of ingredients, including chicken, veal, and rabbit, and is classically paired with brown butter for dressing fresh pasta.

THYME Earthy and warm, thyme, a relative of mint, pairs well with other herbs, balancing out the flavors rather than overpowering them. Thyme goes well with mushrooms, dried beans, tomato sauces, and poultry and is a common addition to marinades.

With roots in northern Italy, this stew, prepared *alla cacciatora*, or "hunter's wife style," has numerous regional variations based on the concept of braising chicken in tomatoes or wine or both, along with aromatics and vegetables. Here, the tomatoes are spiked with olives and capers to create a delicious, piquant sauce.

CHICKEN CACCIATORE

¼ cup canola oil

1 3–4-lb. chicken, cut into 8 pieces

Kosher salt and freshly ground black pepper, to taste

½ cup flour

1 tsp. finely chopped fresh rosemary

2 cloves garlic, finely chopped

1 bay leaf

1 medium carrot, peeled and cut into ¼″ pieces

1 medium red bell pepper, stemmed, seeded, and thinly sliced

1 small yellow onion, thinly sliced

⅔ cup white wine

1 28-oz. can whole peeled tomatoes, crushed by hand

½ cup Gaeta olives, pitted and lightly smashed

¼ cup capers, drained

1 tbsp. finely chopped fresh flat-leaf parsley

SERVES 6–8

1 Heat oil in a 12″ skillet over medium-high. Season chicken with salt and pepper and dredge in flour. Working in batches, cook chicken until browned, 10–12 minutes; transfer to a plate. Add rosemary, garlic, bay leaf, carrot, bell pepper, and onion to skillet; cook until golden, 6–8 minutes. Add wine; cook, stirring and scraping browned bits from bottom of skillet, until reduced by half, about 3 minutes.

2 Return chicken to skillet and add tomatoes; bring to a simmer. Cook, covered, until chicken is tender, about 30 minutes. Uncover and stir in olives, capers, and parsley. Transfer chicken to a serving platter and spoon sauce over top.

Beating an egg yolk into this dish's garlicky herb sauce thickens it and gives it a special velvety texture and appearance. The recipe originated with a group of nuns living at the base of Sicily's volcanic Mount Etna and incorporates several of that island's specialties: anchovies, capers, and lemon.

CAPER-BRAISED CHICKEN WITH GARLIC & HERBED POTATOES

1	salt-packed whole anchovy
¼–½	cup Pantelleria or other salt-packed capers
6	large cloves garlic (2 peeled, 4 unpeeled)
¼	cup extra-virgin olive oil
8	small waxy potatoes, parboiled and quartered
	Kosher salt and freshly ground black pepper, to taste
2	large sprigs fresh rosemary
2	large sprigs fresh sage
1	3–4-lb. chicken, cut into 8 pieces
¼	cup tomato paste
2	tbsp. white wine
¼	cup chicken stock
1	egg yolk
2	tbsp. fresh lemon juice

SERVES 4–6

1 Soak anchovy in a small bowl of warm water for 30 minutes. Meanwhile, soak capers in another bowl of warm water for 10 minutes. Drain capers and repeat soaking process twice more. Drain, then fillet anchovy, discarding bones. Chop anchovy fillet and peeled garlic together to make a fine paste and set aside. Drain capers, coarsely chop, and set aside.

2 Heat 2 tbsp. oil in a 12″ skillet over medium. Add unpeeled garlic and cook, stirring occasionally, for 2–3 minutes. Add potatoes, salt, and pepper and cook until potatoes are lightly browned, about 5 minutes. Add half each of rosemary and sage and cook until garlic and potatoes are tender, 2–3 minutes more. Keep warm.

3 Meanwhile, heat remaining oil in an 8-qt. saucepan over medium-high. Season chicken with salt and pepper. Working in batches, brown chicken all over, 4–6 minutes; transfer to a plate. Add anchovy mixture and capers to pot and cook, stirring with a wooden spoon, for 20–30 seconds. Add tomato paste and cook, stirring, 30 seconds more. Stir in wine and stock. Return chicken to pot, turning to coat, then add remaining rosemary and sage. Reduce heat to medium-low, cover, and simmer until chicken is cooked through, 20–25 minutes. Using tongs, transfer chicken to a plate.

4 Beat egg yolk and lemon juice together in a bowl. Ladle about ¼ cup sauce from pot into egg mixture, stirring vigorously to prevent egg from curdling, then whisk sauce back into pot. Return chicken to pot, coating pieces with sauce. Serve chicken and sauce on a warm serving platter with potatoes, garlic, and herbs.

This rustic dish from Italy's northeasternmost region, Friuli–Venezia Giulia, centers around guinea hen, a dark-meat bird with a pleasantly gamy flavor. The hen is stuffed with a pork-beef mixture that is wrapped for cooking to maintain its shape. At serving, the stuffing is unwrapped, sliced, and presented with polenta alongside it.

STUFFED GUINEA HEN

FOR THE STUFFING

- 4 oz. ground pork
- 2 oz. ground beef
- 1 egg
- ¼ tsp. freshly grated nutmeg

  Leaves from 5–6 sprigs fresh flat-leaf parsley, finely chopped

  Kosher salt and freshly ground black pepper, to taste

FOR THE GUINEA HEN

- 1 2½-lb. guinea hen

  Kosher salt and freshly ground black pepper, to taste

  Extra-virgin olive oil, for greasing

- 2 cloves garlic
- 1 carrot, peeled and coarsely chopped
- 1 rib celery, coarsely chopped
- 1 yellow onion, chopped
- 2 sprigs fresh rosemary
- 6–8 sprigs fresh thyme
- 1 cup white wine
- 2 tbsp. flour
- 1 cup chicken stock

  Polenta, for serving

SERVES 2

1 Make the stuffing: Mix together pork, beef, egg, nutmeg, parsley, salt, and pepper. Form into a log, then wrap tightly in plastic wrap to keep its shape.

2 Make the guinea hen: Heat oven to 450°F. Rinse guinea hen and dry with paper towels; season inside and out with salt and pepper. Place wrapped stuffing into cavity and truss bird with butcher's twine. Lightly oil a medium roasting pan and arrange garlic, carrot, celery, onion, rosemary, and half of thyme in center. Put guinea hen on top of vegetables and roast until bird is browned, 15–20 minutes. Reduce heat to 375°F, pour wine into pan, and continue roasting for about 45 minutes.

3 Transfer bird to a platter. Untruss, then remove stuffing from cavity, unwrap, and cut into slices about ¾″ thick; arrange on platter and set aside. Remove vegetables from pan and discard, then stir flour into pan drippings and add remaining thyme sprigs. Cook over medium for 2–3 minutes, then add stock. Increase heat to high and reduce for 3 minutes. Strain sauce, discarding thyme sprigs. Serve guinea hen and sausage stuffing with sauce and polenta.

Vin santo, a dessert wine that originated in Tuscany but is now found throughout Italy, adds sweetness to this rustic roast chicken dish and provides a perfect base for the garlicky, herb-infused pan sauce.

HERBED ROAST CHICKEN WITH VIN SANTO

3   tbsp. extra-virgin olive oil

1   tbsp. finely chopped
    fresh oregano, plus 0 sprigs

1   tbsp. finely chopped
    fresh rosemary, plus 3 sprigs

1   tbsp. finely chopped
    fresh thyme, plus 3 sprigs

2   cloves garlic, finely chopped,
    plus 3 cloves unpeeled

    Kosher salt and freshly
    ground black pepper,
    to taste

1   3–4-lb. chicken

2   cups vin santo or marsala

SERVES 4-6

Heat oven to 425°F. Combine oil, chopped herbs and garlic, salt, and pepper in a bowl. Slide fingers under skin of chicken breast to create a pocket. Rub mixture over and under skin and inside body cavity. Tie legs together using butcher's twine and tuck wings under back. Place chicken in a roasting pan along with herb sprigs and unpeeled garlic cloves and add wine. Roast until browned and an instant-read thermometer inserted into thickest part of thigh reads 165°F, about 1 hour. Transfer chicken to a cutting board; let rest 10 minutes before carving. Strain sauce through a fine-mesh sieve and serve with chicken.

This recipe comes from the restaurant Da Paolino in Sorrento, a lovely town on the Amalfi coast. The area prides itself on its lemons, and in this classic pairing, both the fruit and its fragrant leaves are grilled with the meat. Look for lemon leaves at farmers' markets.

GRILLED CHICKEN WITH LEMON LEAVES

4 large skin-on, boneless chicken breasts (about 3 lb. total)

1 tbsp. finely chopped fresh rosemary

1 tsp. chile flakes

Kosher salt and freshly ground black pepper, to taste

5 lemons, thinly sliced and seeded

36 large lemon leaves

Lemon wedges, for serving

SERVES 4

1 Lay 1 chicken breast half, skin side up, between 2 large sheets of plastic wrap and, using the flat side of a meat mallet, pound out evenly until chicken is ½" thick. Remove from plastic wrap, place on a large plate, and repeat with remaining chicken.

2 Heat a grill pan over medium until hot but not smoking. Sprinkle rosemary, chile flakes, salt, and pepper over both sides of chicken. Grill chicken, skin side down, until golden and crisp, about 5–6 minutes. Flip chicken over and continue to grill until golden on second side, about 3 minutes. Transfer chicken, skin side up, to a clean plate. Top each breast with 3 overlapping slices of lemon and 2 lemon leaves lined up lengthwise. Carefully flip chicken, so leaf side is down, onto grill pan and cook until lemons are lightly browned, leaves are softened and slightly charred, and chicken is cooked through, 2–3 minutes more.

3 Arrange remaining lemon slices and leaves between 4 plates. Top each with a grilled chicken breast and one-quarter of grilled lemons and leaves. Serve with lemon wedges.

In Marcella Hazan's words, this simple dish "starts out as two before becoming one." Instead of being braised in the rustic tomato sauce, the lamb chops are seared separately and put to the side while the sauce cooks. The result is chops that remain pink and juicy.

CALABRIAN-STYLE LAMB CHOPS

1 large red bell pepper

8 rib lamb chops, each about 1″ thick

Kosher salt and freshly ground black pepper, to taste

2 tbsp. extra-virgin olive oil

½ cup chopped yellow onion

1 28-oz. can whole peeled tomatoes, crushed by hand

¼ cup green olives in brine, pitted and coarsely chopped

3 tbsp. finely chopped fresh flat-leaf parsley

SERVES 4

1 Cut bell pepper lengthwise along creases; stem, seed, and peel with a swivel blade vegetable peeler. Cut into 1½″ squares.

2 Season lamb with salt and pepper. Heat oil in a 12″ skillet over high; cook lamb, turning, until browned, 6–8 minutes. Set lamb aside. Add onion to pan and cook until golden, 5–7 minutes; add tomatoes and cook 5 minutes. Add bell pepper, olives, parsley, salt, and pepper. Reduce heat to medium and cook, stirring occasionally, until bell pepper is tender, 6–8 minutes. Return lamb to skillet and cook until warmed through, 5 minutes more. Transfer lamb to a serving platter and top with sauce.

Roasted, grilled, braised, or fried, rabbit, or *coniglio,* is a popular menu item in almost every Italian region. Here, the lean, flavorful meat is cooked simply—first browned and then braised in an aromatic sauce.

RABBIT BRAISED IN RED WINE

1   750-ml bottle red wine

¼   cup red wine vinegar

2¼ tbsp. sugar

1   2–3-lb. rabbit, cut into 8 pieces (see sidebar)

Kosher salt and freshly ground black pepper, to taste

¼   cup flour

¼   cup extra-virgin olive oil

10 garlic cloves, crushed, plus 6 whole garlic cloves

16 fresh sage leaves

6   fresh rosemary sprigs

Crusty bread, for serving

SERVES 4

1 Heat oven to 350°F. Whisk wine, vinegar, and sugar in a bowl; set aside. Season rabbit with salt and pepper and dredge in flour; shake off excess. Heat oil in a 12″ skillet over medium. Cook rabbit, turning once, until browned on all sides, about 6 minutes. Transfer rabbit to a 9″ x 13″ baking dish.

2 Add crushed garlic to the skillet; cook, stirring constantly, until golden brown, 3–4 minutes. Pour wine mixture into skillet and bring to a boil, stirring and scraping up browned bits from bottom of pan. Pour sauce over rabbit. Scatter sage, rosemary, and whole garlic cloves over top. Cover and braise in oven until tender, 45 minutes. Uncover, raise heat to 450°F, and continue cooking, basting rabbit until sauce is thickened, about 25 minutes more. Season with salt and pepper. Serve with bread.

PREPARING RABBIT

Rabbit takes particularly well to moist cooking methods, such as braises and stews. In Italy, you'll find rabbit braised in red wine and herbs, served atop fettuccine, or cooked with tomatoes into a hearty ragù.

You can probably blame the animals themselves for their ubiquity in Italy, since Italian rabbits are typically bigger and richer tasting than their American counterparts. However, the game meat is growing in popularity in the United States, and many specialty butchers now carry rabbit, which is typically sold whole. Here are some tips for cutting one down to size. These steps will yield eight individual pieces: four leg pieces of equal size, two pieces of meat from along the lower loin, and two pieces attached to the backbone.

1 Lay the rabbit on its back and take hold of one hind leg. Cut along the seam where the leg joins the body, moving inward to separate the thigh from the tailbone.

2 Repeat on the front leg on the same side; cut flush against the neck bone to remove this leg. Repeat for both legs on the opposite side.

3 Locate the rib bones with your fingers. Counting two bones up from the tail, cut between the second and third rib bones on either side to release two flaps of meat; this is the loin. With a cleaver and a firm chop, remove the rib-cage section from the rest of the rabbit, cutting through the backbone. Discard.

4 Sever and discard the tailbone where it meets the rabbit's saddle.

5 With the cleaver, cut the saddle in half lengthwise, through the backbone.

Truffle season in Umbria lasts from October to March, during which time the pungent fungi are used to add a touch of luxury to everything in sight. A favorite preparation: Pan-fried veal cutlets bathed in a buttery, truffle-rich sauce.

PAN-FRIED VEAL WITH TRUFFLES & MUSHROOM SAUCE

⅓   cup extra-virgin olive oil

2   lb. veal cutlets, pounded ⅓″ thick

   Kosher salt and freshly ground black pepper, to taste

12   white button mushrooms, thinly sliced

1½   tbsp. finely chopped fresh rosemary

½   tsp. chile flakes

6   cloves garlic, thinly sliced

3   tbsp. flour

1¼   cups chicken stock

1   small fresh or canned black truffle

2   tbsp. cold unsalted butter, cubed

SERVES 6

Heat half of oil in a 12″ skillet over medium-high. Season veal with salt and pepper. Working in batches, cook veal, flipping once, until browned, 6–8 minutes, and transfer to a plate. Add remaining oil to skillet and cook mushrooms until browned, 5–7 minutes. Add rosemary, chile flakes, garlic, salt, and pepper and cook 2–3 minutes. Sprinkle in flour and cook 2 minutes. Add stock and bring to a boil. Return veal to skillet and cook until sauce is thickened, 2–3 minutes. Shave half of truffle into skillet and remove from heat. Stir in butter until sauce is emulsified. Transfer to a serving platter. Shave remaining truffle over the top.

This is one of the great centerpieces of Italian cooking and is often served at Passover. Arriving plump and golden brown out of the oven, the roast will fill the kitchen with the aroma of its savory stuffing and pan juices. Carefully slicing between the ribs will ensure that everyone gets a just portion of meat and stuffing, and a rib to savor.

STUFFED VEAL BREAST

2   tbsp. extra-virgin olive oil
2   yellow onions, finely chopped
1   clove garlic, finely chopped
1   lb. pancetta, thinly sliced
7   cups fresh bread crumbs
3   tbsp. finely chopped fresh parsley
1   tbsp. finely chopped fresh sage
1   tbsp. finely chopped fresh thyme
1   tbsp. red wine vinegar
2   eggs, lightly beaten
     Kosher salt and freshly ground black pepper, to taste
6   carrots, peeled and sliced
4   leeks, white part only, rinsed and quartered
1   whole veal breast, 12–14 lb., cut with pocket
2   cups white wine

SERVES 8-10

1 Heat oven to 325°F. Heat oil in a 12″ skillet over medium and cook onions and garlic until soft, 15 minutes. Add ¼ of pancetta and cook until brown, about 6 minutes. Stir in bread crumbs, parsley, sage, thyme, vinegar, eggs, salt, pepper, and 2 tbsp. water. Set stuffing aside.

2 Place carrots and leeks in a large roasting pan. Season veal with salt and pepper, fill pocket with stuffing, and place meat in pan on top of vegetables. Arrange remaining pancetta on top. Cook, uncovered, for 2 hours, adding water if necessary. Transfer veal to a platter and discard carrots and leeks. Skim fat from pan juices, deglaze with wine over medium, stirring and scraping up browned bits from bottom of pan, and reduce sauce by half. Serve veal with sauce.

A Venetian classic, liver and onions are here sautéed with nothing but a little bit of salt. The result: sweet, deeply browned onions and crispy bits of liver topped with a decadent parsley-butter sauce. This recipe, from Harry's Bar in Venice, is considered by many to be the city's best.

CALF'S LIVER & ONIONS

2   lb. calf's liver, trimmed and thin membrane peeled

6   tbsp. extra-virgin olive oil

6   small yellow onions, halved and very thinly sliced

    Kosher salt and freshly ground black pepper, to taste

3   tbsp. unsalted butter

    Leaves from ½ bunch fresh flat-leaf parsley, chopped

    Grilled polenta, for serving

SERVES 6

1 Cut liver lengthwise into 4 long pieces, then, using a very sharp knife and pressing the palm of your hand firmly against meat, slice each piece thinly crosswise. Set aside.

2 Heat 4 tbsp. oil in a 12″ skillet over medium. Add onions and cook, stirring frequently, until soft and deep golden brown, about 20 minutes. Using a slotted spoon, transfer onions to a bowl and set aside. Increase heat to medium-high and add remaining oil. Working in batches, add liver and cook, stirring constantly with a wooden spoon, until brown and crispy on the edges, 3–5 minutes. When all of the liver is cooked, return liver to the pan, season with salt and pepper, and add reserved onions and any juices. Cook for 2 minutes, stirring and turning liver and onions constantly while shaking skillet over heat. Transfer to a serving platter and keep warm.

3 Add butter to skillet. Stir and scrape up any browned bits on bottom of pan as butter melts. Remove skillet from heat and stir in parsley. Spoon butter and parsley over liver and onions. Serve with grilled polenta.

In autumn, markets in Italy begin to fill with broccoli rabe and broccolini, both perfect accompaniments to fatty sausage. Here tender broccolini florets get added at the very end just to soften, joining a stewy combination of sweet Italian sausages, carrots, celery, and hearty, creamy beans.

SAUSAGE WITH BROCCOLINI & CRANBERRY BEANS

2 tbsp. extra-virgin olive oil

¾ lb. sweet Italian sausages

1 yellow onion, chopped

2 tbsp. finely chopped fresh flat-leaf parsley

2 ribs celery, chopped

2 small carrots, peeled and chopped

3 cloves garlic, finely chopped

2 sprigs fresh oregano

2 cups dried cranberry beans or white beans, soaked overnight and drained

1 lb. broccolini, trimmed and cut into 2″ lengths

Kosher salt and freshly ground black pepper, to taste

SERVES 6

1 Heat oil in a 12″ skillet over medium-high. Add sausages and cook, turning until browned, about 15 minutes. Remove sausages from pan, cut into thick slices, and set aside.

2 Reduce heat to medium-low. Add onion and cook until soft, about 20 minutes. Add parsley, celery, and carrots and cook, stirring occasionally, for 10 minutes. Add garlic and oregano and cook 2 minutes more. Return sausage pieces to skillet. Add beans and 3 cups water and bring to a boil. Reduce heat to medium-low and cook, covered, until beans are just tender, about 40 minutes. Uncover, raise heat to medium-high, and reduce liquid by half, about 10 minutes. Add broccolini, stir well, cover, and cook until tender, 5–7 minutes. Season with salt and pepper, then transfer to a large bowl and serve.

A whole pork loin enclosed in a whole pork belly, this porchetta is an ideal special-occasion roast—the outside crisps, and underneath there are layers of tender meat, both lean and fatty. To keep the meat moist, tightly wrap it in plastic wrap and then aluminum foil before roasting.

PORCHETTA

3   tbsp. grated lemon zest

2   tbsp. crushed fennel seeds

12   cloves garlic, finely chopped

1   12–14-lb. skin-on pork belly

1   3–5-lb. trimmed pork loin

     Kosher salt and freshly ground black pepper, to taste

1½   tsp. baking soda

SERVES 10–14

1 Combine lemon zest, fennel seeds, and garlic in a small bowl and set aside. Lay pork belly skin side down with a long edge parallel to you. Arrange pork loin along center, widthwise. Trim away overhanging ends of loin. Fold belly over loin. Trim pork belly meat and fat, but not skin, along one side, so when belly is wrapped around loin, trimmed skin flap covers seam of belly. (Flap will help seal roast when rolled.) Make ½"-deep slashes all over inside of belly. Rub belly and loin with lemon-and-garlic mixture and season with salt and pepper. Return loin to center of belly. Wrap belly around loin, sealing it with skin flap. Tie roast at 1" intervals with butcher's twine. Wrap roast with plastic wrap and then foil. Refrigerate the pork, fully wrapped, for at least 24 hours or up to 3 days.

2 Transfer meat, still wrapped, to a rimmed baking sheet fitted with a rack. Let come to room temperature, about 2 hours. Heat oven to 325°F and arrange an oven rack in bottom third of oven. Cook porchetta until an instant-read thermometer inserted into center of roast reads 130°F, about 3 hours. Carefully remove foil and plastic wrap from roast and pat dry. Rub baking soda on skin. Set oven to broil, place baking sheet under broiler, and continue cooking porchetta, turning frequently, until skin is crisp all over, about 20 minutes. Let meat rest for 15 minutes before carving.

This pan-seared pork loin comes from Villa Roncalli, a historic inn in the Umbrian town of Foligno. It's a full-flavored partner for the area's famed red wine, the robust and tannic sagrantino. The dish's aromatics are provided by pungent juniper berries—the key flavoring of gin—and fresh herbs.

PORK WITH JUNIPER BERRIES & POTATOES

FOR THE POTATOES

1/3	cup extra-virgin olive oil
1	lb. russet potatoes, peeled and cut into 1" pieces
10	oz. green beans, trimmed
1½	tbsp. finely chopped sage
3	cloves garlic, finely chopped
	Kosher salt and freshly ground black pepper, to taste

FOR THE PORK

3	tbsp. lard or extra-virgin olive oil
2	oz. guanciale or pancetta, finely chopped
1	lb. pork tenderloin
	Kosher salt and freshly ground black pepper, to taste
1	tbsp. juniper berries
4	sprigs fresh rosemary
3	sprigs fresh thyme
2	bay leaves
2	cloves garlic, finely chopped
2	sprigs flowering fennel heads (optional)
1	cup white wine
1	cup chicken stock

SERVES 4

1 Make the potatoes: Heat oil in a 12" skillet over medium-high. Cook potatoes until golden, 10–12 minutes. Stir in green beans, sage, garlic, salt, and pepper. Reduce heat to medium and cook, covered, until potatoes are tender, 6–8 minutes. Transfer to a bowl and keep warm.

2 Make the pork: Wipe skillet clean and melt lard over medium-high. Cook guanciale until crisp, 2–3 minutes. Using a slotted spoon, transfer guanciale to a plate. Season pork with salt and pepper; add to skillet and cook, turning as needed, until browned, 8–10 minutes.

3 Add juniper berries, rosemary, thyme, bay leaves, garlic, and fennel, if using; cook 1–2 minutes. Add wine and cook, stirring and scraping browned bits from bottom of pan, until almost evaporated,

12–15 minutes. Add stock and bring to a boil. Reduce heat to medium; cook, partially covered, until an instant-read thermometer inserted into pork reads 145°F. Transfer pork to a plate and let rest for 5 minutes; slice ½" thick and divide between plates. Simmer sauce over medium until thickened, 10–12 minutes. Discard herbs, stir in reserved guanciale, and season with salt and pepper; spoon over pork. Serve with potatoes and green beans.

VEGETABLES
& SIDES

When making this delicious dish, resist the urge to flip the squash too soon—you want each side to be a nice, caramelized brown. For even deeper color, and extra crispy bits, feel free to slice the squash thinner than called for in the recipe.

ROASTED SQUASH AGRODOLCE

½ cup golden raisins

2 lb. winter squash, peeled, seeded, and cut into ½" wedges

3 tbsp. extra-virgin olive oil

Kosher salt and freshly ground black pepper, to taste

½ cup balsamic vinegar

3 tbsp. sugar

1 tsp. chile flakes

¼ cup toasted hazelnuts, coarsely chopped

Fresh basil leaves, to garnish

SERVES 4

1 Put raisins in a small bowl; cover with hot water and let soften for 30 minutes.

2 Heat oven to 400°F. Toss squash, oil, salt, and pepper on a baking sheet and roast until golden and tender, 25 minutes. Transfer squash to a serving platter and keep warm.

3 Meanwhile, heat vinegar, sugar, chile flakes, and ¼ cup water in a 2-qt. saucepan over medium-high; simmer until thickened, 5 minutes, and season with salt. Cook, stirring, until sauce thickens, 2–3 minutes; pour over squash. Garnish with raisins, hazelnuts, and basil leaves.

AGRODOLCE

Used to describe a sweet-and-sour flavor, the word *agrodolce* is typically applied to sauces and marinades that are made by combining vinegar and sugar or honey and reducing the mixture until slightly thickened. Popular in southern Italy and especially in Sicily, it is a classic flavoring for cipollini onions, where the syrup both tames the onions' bite and complements their caramelized sweetness. Similar in flavor to a French *gastrique, agrodolce* is often used as a marinade or glaze for pork chops, lamb steaks, and chicken thighs, or to add bold flavor to vegetable-based dishes, such as the one at left and Sicilian Eggplant & Tuna Salad on page 62.

Although traditionally roasted directly in the embers of a charcoal fire until charred and tender, these spicy southern Italian–style artichokes are equally satisfying when roasted in a very hot oven.

ROASTED ARTICHOKES

1½   cups extra-virgin olive oil

1½   cups white wine

2   tbsp. dried oregano

2–3   tsp. chile flakes

12   cloves garlic, finely chopped

Kosher salt and freshly ground black pepper, to taste

6   globe artichokes, stemmed

SERVES 6

Heat oven to 500°F. In a bowl, whisk together oil, wine, oregano, chile flakes, garlic, salt, and pepper and set aside. Cut 1″ off top of each artichoke and gently pull leaves apart to open artichokes. Place artichokes standing up in a small roasting pan or dish large enough to hold them in one layer. Pour oil mixture over each artichoke, making sure it reaches in between all leaves. Cover with aluminum foil and bake for 45 minutes. Uncover and and continue baking, basting often with juices, until browned and tender, about 30 minutes more. Let cool for 10 minutes before serving warm with pan juices.

WORKING WITH ARTICHOKES

Whether you're partial to the baby variety, the larger, leafier kind, the tender hearts, or the fleshy bases of the leaves, there are countless ways to enjoy artichokes.

Each region of Italy has a signature dish featuring this edible thistle. Artichokes are most commonly roasted or boiled, but the Romans have perfected *carciofi alla giudia*, or Jewish-style artichokes, which involves frying whole artichokes until brown and crisp. In other regions of Italy, you'll find stuffed baked artichokes brimming with fresh bread crumbs, pine nuts, anchovies, and olives; braised baby artichokes; and brined artichoke hearts, which regularly appear on antipasti platters, scattered atop pizza and focaccia, and tucked inside panini.

To prepare artichokes for cooking, trim about 1 inch off both the thorny top and the fibrous stalk of the bud. You'll want to work quickly and have a bowl of lemon water on hand for soaking the trimmed artichoke, since the vegetable turns brown when cut into.

The roots of this recipe are in the region of Emilia-Romagna, often considered the ancestral home of northern Italian cooking. Choose smooth and firm eggplants with glossy skin. Smaller eggplants are generally sweeter than larger ones. Salting the eggplant slices will draw out any bitterness and excess moisture; let salted slices stand for 30 minutes, then blot with a paper towel before breading and frying.

FRIED EGGPLANT WITH ROASTED TOMATOES & BASIL

2 pints cherry tomatoes

¼ cup extra-virgin olive oil, plus more for drizzling

Kosher salt and freshly ground black pepper, to taste

½ cup flour

4 eggs, beaten

1½ cups dried bread crumbs (page 33)

2 small eggplants (about 8 oz. each), cut crosswise into ⅓"-thick slices

Canola oil, for frying

¼ cup fresh basil leaves

½ cup grated Parmigiano-Reggiano

SERVES 4

1 Heat oven to 400°F. Toss tomatoes, olive oil, salt, and pepper on a baking sheet and roast until blistered and soft, 10 minutes. Transfer tomatoes to a bowl and mash lightly; keep warm.

2 Place flour, eggs, and bread crumbs in separate shallow dishes. Working with 1 slice at a time, dredge eggplant slices in flour, then dip in eggs; coat in bread crumbs and transfer to a plate. Heat 2" canola oil in a 6-qt. saucepan until a deep-fry thermometer reads 350°F. Working in batches, fry eggplant until golden, 3–4 minutes.

3 To serve, divide eggplant between plates, top with tomatoes, basil, and Parmigiano and drizzle with olive oil.

Cerignola olives, a large green variety grown primarily in Puglia, are known for their fleshiness and mild salinity. Here, they deliver those qualities and a buttery flavor to a dish of mushrooms and green beans.

PORCINI WITH GREEN BEANS & OLIVES

Kosher salt and freshly ground black pepper, to taste

½ lb. green beans, trimmed

6 tbsp. unsalted butter

2 lb. porcini mushrooms, quartered

3 cloves garlic, finely chopped

½ cup Cerignola olives, pitted and halved

¼ cup sherry vinegar

Lemon wedges, for serving

SERVES 6

1 In a large saucepan of salted boiling water, cook beans until tender, 3–4 minutes. Using a slotted spoon, transfer to a bowl of ice water; drain and pat dry.

2 Heat butter in a 12″ skillet over medium-high and cook porcini and garlic until golden, 6–8 minutes. Add beans, olives, vinegar, salt, and pepper and cook 2 minutes more, until beans are heated through. Transfer to a serving platter and serve with lemon wedges.

Rome is just as well known for its *contorni* (side dishes) as for its exquisite pasta dishes. In this classic Roman pairing, sweet peas are richly flavored by salty prosciutto as well as the pork's rendered fat.

FRESH PEAS WITH PROSCIUTTO

¼ cup extra-virgin olive oil

2 oz. prosciutto, coarsely chopped

1 small white onion, finely chopped

1 lb. fresh or frozen green peas

Kosher salt and freshly ground black pepper, to taste

SERVES 4

Heat oil in a 12″ skillet over medium. Add prosciutto and onion and cook until onion is soft and prosciutto begins to crisp, 6–8 minutes. Add peas and 1 tbsp. water and cook until hot, about 3 minutes. Season with salt and pepper.

PAIRING CONTORNI

The vegetable dishes that accompany *secondi* (main dishes) are known as *contorni* ("contours"), because they enhance the meal and complete the menu.

These flavorful preparations reflect the season's best produce and complement the meat, fish, poultry, pizza, or pasta at the table. They can be as simple as fresh greens sautéed in olive oil or as elaborate as a grape-embellished focaccia. Here are some tips for pairing contorni with secondi.

STARCHES Polenta, potatoes, and focaccia are best served alongside saucy dishes. As is the tradition in Italy, each dish is presented in a separate bowl or platter for passing family-style at the table.

VEGETABLES Hearty meat and fish dishes are lightened up with a side of vegetables. Choose a vegetable side based on what is available at the market and what the flavor profile of the secondi includes. If the secondi features bold, heavy flavors, such as garlic, rich cheese, and spicy peppers, consider contorni dressed with contrasting brighter flavors, such as fresh basil, citrus, and capers.

DOP INGREDIENTS

The acronym DOP stands for *Denominazione di Origine Protetta,* which translates to "Protected Designation of Origin (PDO)." As the first country to embrace the slow food movement, which, among other things, defends regional cuisine and local foods, Italy is extremely protective of its artisanal products, and the DOP certification ensures the quality of various categories of food. It is a guarantee by the government to the consumer that the food being purchased is grown and made by local farmers and artisans using traditional methods and working in specific geographical areas. It's worth seeking out DOP products to taste the true culinary heritage of the many regions of Italy. Here are a few of the most famous products carrying the DOP seal.

 SAN MARZANO TOMATOES Hand harvested in Campania, these tomatoes (shown opposite) have a bittersweet flavor and firm pulp and are the key to vibrant pizza and pasta sauces.

 OLIVE OIL One of the most traditionally produced ingredients in the country, olive oil has more DOP designations than any other Italian specialty. Some regions have several DOP oils from various areas.

 **BALSAMIC VINEGAR** DOP balsamic vinegar from Modena and Reggio Emilia, in Emilia-Romagna, is aged 12 years or more, resulting in a particularly rich taste and thick consistency that is perfect for drizzling on a variety of foods, from asparagus to steak to strawberries.

 PARMIGIANO-REGGIANO Italy's iconic grating cheese is designated in Emilia-Romagna and Lombardy, where it must age for a minimum of 16 months. In addition to enjoying it as the perfect pasta topper, Italians like to eat the salty shards with fresh and dried fruits.

The key to this simple recipe is using three types of tomatoes and giving each of them individual attention. The result is a bouquet of flavors and textures, from sweet, burst-in-your mouth cherry tomatoes to a molten broth fragrant with herbs that begs to be mopped up with Italian bread.

OVEN-STEWED TOMATOES

4	large tomatoes
1	15-oz. can whole peeled tomatoes
4	cloves garlic, finely chopped
3	tbsp. extra-virgin olive oil
6	sprigs fresh thyme
	Kosher salt and freshly ground black pepper, to taste
12	red cherry tomatoes
12	yellow cherry tomatoes
1	handful fresh basil leaves, torn into pieces, to garnish

SERVES 4

Heat oven to 375°F. Bring a medium pot of water to a boil and blanch large tomatoes for 15–30 seconds, then remove with a slotted spoon. Nick skin of each tomato with a knife tip, then peel and core. Arrange large tomatoes and canned tomatoes in a large baking dish. Sprinkle garlic over and around tomatoes. Drizzle with oil, thyme, salt, and pepper. Bake tomatoes for 30 minutes, basting several times. Add cherry tomatoes and continue baking, basting once, until all tomatoes are heated through and cherry tomatoes just burst, 10–15 minutes more. Taste and adjust seasoning. Divide tomatoes and broth between 4 bowls. Garnish with basil.

This greens-and-beans dish, known simply as *verdure con fagioli,* has a souplike consistency. Sautéed aromatics—celery, carrot, onion, and garlic—are combined with wilted greens and tender beans and then simmered in stock to create a hearty, brothy, protein-rich classic.

SWISS CHARD WITH BORLOTTI BEANS

2 cups dried borlotti or cranberry beans, soaked overnight and drained

Kosher salt and freshly ground black pepper, to taste

7 lb. Swiss chard, leaves and tender stems coarsely chopped

⅓ cup extra-virgin olive oil

1 tsp. chile flakes

12 cloves garlic, coarsely chopped

4 ribs celery, cut into ¼" pieces

3 carrots, peeled and cut into ¼" pieces

1 yellow onion, cut into ¼" pieces

2 cups chicken or vegetable stock

SERVES 6

1 Put beans and 6 cups water in a 6-qt. saucepan and bring to a boil. Reduce heat to medium-low and cook, covered, until beans are tender, about 2 hours. Drain beans and set aside.

2 Fill a saucepan with salted water and bring to a boil. Add chard and cook until leaves are wilted and stems are tender, 4–6 minutes. Drain and transfer chard to an ice bath until chilled, then drain and squeeze dry. Add ¼ cup oil and the chile flakes to saucepan over medium and cook garlic, celery, carrots, and onion until golden, 8–10 minutes. Add reserved beans and chard, the stock, salt, and pepper and simmer until stock is slightly reduced, 6–8 minutes. Transfer to a serving dish and drizzle with remaining oil.

During the colder months, you will find *finocchio* (fennel) stacked in markets across Italy. In this recipe, its licorice-like flavor mellows as it cooks, allowing the natural sweetness of the vegetable to play against the creaminess of the milk.

FENNEL BAKED IN MILK

4   cups milk

4   tbsp. unsalted butter

3   bulbs fennel, trimmed
     and cut into ½″ wedges

1   tsp. fennel seeds, crushed

     Kosher salt and freshly
     ground black pepper,
     to taste

1   cup grated Parmigiano-
     Reggiano

SERVES 4–6

Heat oven to 475°F. Combine milk, 2 tbsp. butter, and fennel in a 4-qt. saucepan over medium-high and cook, stirring occasionally, until fennel is just tender, 30–45 minutes. Add fennel seeds, salt, and pepper. Using a slotted spoon, transfer fennel to a 2-qt. oval baking dish. Dot with remaining butter. Pour 1 cup milk mixture over fennel, sprinkle with Parmigiano, and bake until golden brown and bubbly, about 20 minutes.

A savory summer pie with a base of ricotta and eggs is the answer to an abundant vegetable harvest. This version from Piedmont is made with zucchini, but other vegetables can be substituted, such as bell peppers, eggplants, or tomatoes—whatever you have on hand.

ZUCCHINI & SHALLOT PIE

¼ cup extra-virgin olive oil

2 cloves garlic, thinly sliced

1 shallot, thinly sliced

6 zucchini, thinly sliced

½ cup grated Pecorino Romano

½ cup homemade (page 18) or store-bought ricotta

½ cup coarsely chopped fresh flat-leaf parsley

4 eggs, beaten

Kosher salt and freshly ground black pepper, to taste

Unsalted butter, for greasing

3 tbsp. dried bread crumbs (page 33)

SERVES 6

1 Heat oil in a 6-qt. saucepan over medium-high. Cook garlic and shallot until golden, 4–6 minutes. Add zucchini and cook, stirring occasionally, until golden, about 15 minutes. Transfer to a bowl and let cool. Stir in Pecorino, ricotta, parsley, eggs, salt, and pepper.

2 Heat oven to 350°F. Grease a 10″ pie plate and coat with bread crumbs. Spread zucchini mixture evenly over top; bake until golden and slightly puffed, 40–45 minutes. Serve hot or at room temperature.

The bright, briny flavors of anchovies and capers, combined with fresh lemon juice and parsley, lend a refreshing salinity to this dish, balancing the sweeter caramelized notes of the roasted cauliflower.

ROASTED CAULIFLOWER
WITH ANCHOVY DRESSING

1   head cauliflower,
    cut into florets

¾   cup extra-virgin olive oil

    Kosher salt and freshly
    ground black pepper,
    to taste

⅓   cup large capers, drained

3   tbsp. fresh lemon juice

6   anchovies, mashed
    into a paste

¼   cup fresh flat-leaf
    parsley leaves

SERVES 6

1 Heat broiler. Place cauliflower florets on a baking sheet and toss with ¼ cup oil, the salt, and pepper; broil, 4″ from heat, stirring as needed, until cauliflower is chewy and slightly charred, about 10 minutes. Transfer to a serving platter and keep warm.

2 Meanwhile, heat ¼ cup oil in a 10″ skillet over medium-high. Fry capers until crisp, 6–8 minutes. Using a slotted spoon, transfer to paper towels to drain. Whisk remaining oil, lemon juice, and anchovies in a bowl; drizzle over cauliflower. Sprinkle capers and parsley leaves on top.

As this fluffy, oil-slathered dough bakes, the red and green grapes dotting its surface burst, releasing their sweet juices into the bread. It's a favorite recipe of Emidio Pepe, the celebrated Abruzzese winemaker.

ABRUZZO-STYLE GRAPE FOCACCIA

⅓ cup extra virgin olive oil, plus more for greasing and brushing

1 cup milk

5 cups flour

2 tsp. kosher salt

1 ¼-oz. package active dry yeast

6 oz. seedless green and/or red grapes

Maldon flake sea salt, to taste

SERVES 10–12

1 Grease a 13" x 18" rimmed baking sheet and set aside. Heat milk and 1 cup water in a 1-qt. saucepan over medium until an instant-read thermometer reads 115°F. Pulse flour, kosher salt, and yeast in a food processor to combine. With the motor running, slowly add milk mixture and oil; mix until a smooth dough forms. Transfer dough to a lightly greased bowl and cover loosely with plastic wrap. Set in a warm spot to rise until doubled in size, about 1 hour.

2 Transfer dough to prepared baking sheet and, using your fingers, spread dough out until it completely covers bottom of pan. Using your fingertips, press dough all over to form dimples. Press grapes into dough 1½–2" apart. Brush dough with oil and sprinkle with sea salt. Let sit, uncovered, until puffed, about 45 minutes.

3 Heat oven to 400°F. Bake focaccia until golden brown, about 25 minutes. Let cool slightly before cutting into pieces and serving.

DESSERTS

These chewy almond meringue cookies originated in Sicily, where some of the world's best pine nuts are cultivated. The cookies are as popular in their homeland as they are in Italian-American bakeries.

PINE NUT COOKIES

2 cups whole blanched almonds

½ cup granulated sugar

1 cup confectioners' sugar

3 egg whites, lightly beaten

½ cup pine nuts

MAKES ABOUT 3 DOZEN

Heat oven to 300°F. Combine almonds and granulated sugar in a food processor and process until very finely ground, about 4 minutes. Add confectioners' sugar and egg whites and process until a smooth dough forms. Transfer dough to a piping bag fitted with a ½" round tip and pipe 1½" mounds of dough 2" apart on parchment paper–lined baking sheets. Gently press 10–12 pine nuts on top of each mound so they adhere. Bake cookies, rotating baking sheets top to bottom and front to back halfway through cooking, until golden brown, about 25 minutes. Let cool completely before serving.

DIGESTIVI

Everyone likes the *aperitivo* (page 15), a predinner cocktail designed to whet the appetite. Less well known but equally significant is the *digestivo*, a palliative elixir designed to bring the digestive system back in balance after a meal. Here are some of the best and most readily available options in the United States.

AMARI The word *amari* represents a group of bottlings with a characteristic bitterness. Among them are the Fernets, the most famous of which is Fernet-Branca, an intensely bitter herbal liqueur, and the artichoke-based Cynar, which has a dark, murky hue and a sharp vegetal note. Averna, produced in Sicily since 1868, is becoming popular in the United States, perhaps because its maceration of herbs, citrus rinds, and roots is blended with a sugar syrup to cut the bitter herbaceousness.

BAROLO CHINATO This Piedmont specialty is made by steeping botanicals, spices, and the quinine-containing bark of the cinchona tree in the highly prized aged barolo of the region.

GRAPPA This iconic *digestivo* originated as a way to squeeze as much as possible out of wine grapes. The leftover mash of skins, seeds, and stems is distilled to produce a potent brandy. After dinner, many Italians enjoy sipping *caffè corretto*—or coffee that's been "corrected" with grappa.

LIQUEURS These more complex *digestivi* combine fruits, botanicals, and herbs with alcohol and a bit of sugar, resulting in slightly viscous drinks, including *nocino*, made from green walnuts flavored with cloves and lemon peel; *limoncello*, which uses the extra-tart lemon rinds of southern Italy; and Strega, which derives its yellow hue from saffron.

These cream-filled cookies are tall and wide, so you may want to halve them to make serving easier. They're similar to *baci di dama,* or "lady's kisses," a cookie typical of Piedmont, the hazelnut capital of the world.

HAZELNUT-CREAM SANDWICH COOKIES

FOR THE FILLING

1	cup half-and-half
4	1"-wide strips lemon zest
⅔	cup granulated sugar
2	tbsp. cornstarch
2	egg yolks
¾	cup unsalted butter, softened
¼	cup hazelnut paste

FOR THE COOKIES

3	cups flour, plus more for dusting
¾	cup granulated sugar
1½	tsp. baking powder
¼	tsp. kosher salt
¾	cup cold unsalted butter, cubed
2	eggs
1½	tsp. grated lemon zest
1	cup toasted, chopped hazelnuts
	Confectioners' sugar, for dusting

MAKES ABOUT 9

1 Make the filling: Bring half-and-half and lemon zest to a simmer in a 2-qt. saucepan over medium. Whisk granulated sugar, cornstarch, and egg yolks in a bowl until fluffy. Discard lemon zest and, using a ladle, slowly stir about ½ cup half-and-half into egg mixture until incorporated. Return mixture to pan and cook, whisking constantly, until very thick, about 6 minutes. Transfer pastry cream to a bowl. Place a piece of plastic wrap directly onto surface of cream to prevent a skin from forming and chill for 1 hour.

2 Using an electric hand mixer, beat butter in a bowl until fluffy. Add chilled pastry cream and the hazelnut paste and stir until combined. Cover with plastic wrap and chill until firm, about 1 hour.

3 Make the cookies: Pulse the flour, granulated sugar, baking powder, and salt in a food processor. Add butter, pulsing until pea-size crumbles form. Add eggs and zest and pulse until dough forms. Add 1–2 tbsp. cold water, if necessary, until dough holds together but is not wet. Form dough into 2 discs, wrap in plastic wrap, and chill for 1 hour.

4 Heat oven to 350°F. On a lightly floured surface and using a rolling pin, roll 1 disc dough into a 10" round about ¼" thick. Using a 3" round cutter, cut out cookies and transfer to parchment paper–lined baking sheets. Roll and reuse scraps. Bake cookies, rotating pans top to bottom and front to back halfway through cooking, until just golden, about 20 minutes. Let cookies cool completely.

5 Assemble the cookies: Spread about 1½ tbsp. filling evenly on half of cookies, leaving no border; top with remaining cookies and lightly press together. Roll sides of cookies in chopped hazelnuts. Dust cookies with confectioners' sugar and chill until filling is firm.

These star-shaped cookies are infused with kirsch—a clear, colorless cherry brandy from Germany—and a little cream for extra richness.

CHERRY-ALMOND STAR COOKIES

3 cups flour

2 tsp. baking powder

½ tsp. kosher salt

¾ cup unsalted butter, softened

1 cup sugar

¾ cup almond paste

2 eggs

¼ cup heavy cream

1 tbsp. kirsch

1 tsp. vanilla extract

Maraschino cherries

MAKES ABOUT 4 DOZEN

1 Whisk flour, baking powder, and salt in a bowl and set aside. In another bowl and using an electric hand mixer, cream butter and sugar on medium-high speed until pale and fluffy, about 2 minutes; set aside. In a large bowl, beat almond paste at medium-high speed until smooth; add ¼ of butter mixture and beat until smooth. Add remaining butter mixture and beat until smooth. Add eggs one at a time, beating well after each addition, until evenly combined. Add cream, kirsch, and vanilla and beat until smooth. Add dry ingredients and beat until just combined.

2 Transfer dough to a piping bag fitted with a ½" star tip and pipe 2" mounds of dough 2" apart on parchment paper–lined baking sheets. Halve maraschino cherries and place a cherry half in center of each cookie. Chill cookies for 30 minutes.

3 Heat oven to 375°F. Bake cookies, rotating baking sheets top to bottom and front to back halfway through cooking, until lightly browned, about 14 minutes. Let cool before serving.

ESPRESSO & AFFOGATO

Drunk in the morning, afternoon, and evening whenever a jolt is needed, espresso is one of Italy's greatest gifts to the world. Coffee beans that have been treated to an espresso roast (darker than most roasts for a more intense flavor) and then finely ground are flooded with steaming hot water to release their oils and caffeine into a small cup, or demitasse. This popular drink, which typically contains about three-quarters as much caffeine per serving as a standard cup of American coffee, is seen as the purist expression of coffee beans.

But Italians have found other ways to use espresso beyond the shot, and one of the best of them is a dessert called affogato, or "drowned." It consists of a scoop of ice-cold vanilla gelato doused with a shot of piping-hot espresso. This distant cousin to Italy's more famous confection, tiramisù, which also contains espresso, is the perfect marriage of extreme temperatures, caffeine, and sugar. Add a dash of spiced liqueur for a creamy riff on a caffè corretto.

Cornflakes—both mixed into the batter and coating the exterior—give these crumbly chocolate-chip treats a pleasant crunch. Served at festivals, wineries, and charity bake sales, they are a favorite of residents in the Umbrian hill town of Montefalco.

UMBRIAN SNOWFLAKE COOKIES

2½	cups flour
1	tsp. baking powder
¼	tsp. kosher salt
1¼	cups granulated sugar
½	cup plus 2 tbsp. unsalted butter, softened
3	eggs
6	cups cornflakes (2 cups lightly crushed, 4 cups whole)
¾	cup semisweet chocolate chips
	Confectioners' sugar, for dusting

MAKES 28

Heat oven to 350°F. Whisk flour, baking powder, and salt in a bowl. In another bowl and using an electric hand mixer, cream granulated sugar and butter until fluffy, about 3 minutes. Add eggs one at a time, beating well after each addition. Add dry ingredients and mix until dough forms. Fold in crushed cornflakes and the chocolate chips. Divide dough into 28 balls; roll in whole cornflakes. Space 1" apart on parchment paper–lined baking sheets. Bake until golden and crisp, 20–22 minutes. Let cookies cool and then dust with confectioners' sugar.

This simple dessert (*panna cotta* means "cooked cream") can be dressed up with nearly any kind of fresh fruit or fruit sauce. The custard is noticeably—and pleasantly—spiked, but the bourbon can be reduced by as much as a tablespoon and the dish will still taste great.

BOURBON PANNA COTTA

3 tbsp. plus 1¾ cups heavy cream

1½ tsp. powdered gelatin

¼ cup bourbon

¼ cup sugar

½ split vanilla bean

Fresh fruit, for serving

SERVES 4

Add 3 tbsp. cream to a small bowl and sprinkle with gelatin. Let stand for 10 minutes, then gently stir to dissolve gelatin. Combine remaining cream, bourbon, sugar, and vanilla bean in a 4-qt. saucepan over medium-high and cook, stirring constantly, until hot, 5 minutes. Add gelatin mixture, whisking constantly, and remove from heat. Strain through a fine-mesh sieve and divide evenly between four 6-oz. ramekins. Chill for 12 hours. Unmold onto a plate and serve with fruit.

This indulgent, creamy tart is served at the Trattoria Garga in Florence. The use of English digestives—mildly sweet whole-wheat biscuits—gives the crust an appealing crumbly texture.

FLORENTINE CHOCOLATE TART

FOR THE CRUST

2½ cups finely crushed whole-wheat biscuits

1 tbsp. sugar

4 tbsp. unsalted butter, melted

FOR THE FILLING

16 oz. bittersweet chocolate, chopped

2 cups heavy cream

3 egg yolks

Whipped cream and sliced fresh strawberries, for serving (optional)

MAKES ONE 10" TART

1 Make the crust: Heat oven to 350°F. Combine crushed biscuits and sugar in a bowl. Add butter and stir until well combined. Transfer crumb mixture to a 10" tart pan with a removable bottom. Using your hands, spread mixture out in an even layer, then use your fingertips to press crumb mixture into bottom and up sides of pan to form an even crust. Transfer pan to a baking sheet and bake until crust is set and lightly golden in places, about 15 minutes. Set crust aside until completely cool.

2 Make the filling: Melt chocolate in a heatproof bowl set over a pot of gently simmering water over medium-low, stirring constantly for about 5 minutes.

Remove bowl from heat and set aside. Heat cream in a saucepan over medium until bubbles appear around sides of pan and cream is just about to boil, 8–10 minutes, then remove pan from heat. Meanwhile, in a bowl, whisk egg yolks until smooth. Gradually whisk about ¼ cup hot cream into yolks, then stir mixture into pot of hot cream. Gradually add egg mixture to melted chocolate, stirring until well combined and smooth. Pour filling into prepared crust and set aside to cool, about 30 minutes. Refrigerate until chocolate is completely set, about 3 hours. Remove outer ring of tart pan. Serve with whipped cream and sliced strawberries.

To make the filling for this tart, peaches are simmered with cinnamon and sugar and then mixed with crushed amaretti cookies, which add a nutty almond flavor and a light, almost cakelike texture. The array of decorative cutouts arranged on top gives the tart a festive air.

AMARETTI PEACH TART

FOR THE CRUST

- 1 cup flour, plus more for dusting
- 6 tbsp. cold unsalted butter, plus more for greasing
- 1 tbsp. sugar
- ⅛ tsp. kosher salt
- ¼ cup ice-cold water

FOR THE FILLING

- 3 lb. very ripe peaches, peeled, pitted, and coarsely chopped
- 5 tbsp. sugar
- 1 tbsp. ground cinnamon
- 5½ oz. amaretti cookies, finely crushed

SERVES 8

1 Make the crust: Pulse flour, butter, sugar, and salt in a food processor until pea-size crumbles form. Add water and pulse until dough forms. Flatten dough into a disc and wrap in plastic wrap. Chill for 1 hour.

2 On a lightly floured surface, roll dough into a 15″ round and press into a greased 11″ tart pan with a removable bottom set on a baking sheet; trim edges. Gather and reroll dough scraps and cut into decorative shapes, such as diamonds, leaves, and stars; transfer to baking sheet. Chill for 1 hour.

3 Make the filling: Simmer peaches, sugar, and cinnamon in a 4-qt. saucepan over medium until thick, 40–45 minutes. Stir in cookies and let cool.

4 Heat oven to 425°F. Spread filling over dough and arrange cutouts on top. Bake until crust is golden, 40–45 minutes. Let cool completely before serving.

A heady mixture of olive oil and candied oranges flavors this moist, dense cake. If you like, serve it with vanilla gelato (page 210)—or even a drizzle of fruity extra-virgin olive oil and sprinkle of sea salt.

ORANGE-SCENTED OLIVE OIL CAKE

2	oranges, quartered lengthwise
2⅓	cups granulated sugar
	Unsalted butter, for greasing
2½	cups flour, plus more for dusting
2	tsp. baking powder
1	tsp. baking soda
1	tsp. vanilla extract
4	eggs
6	tbsp. extra-virgin olive oil
¼	cup confectioners' sugar
¼	cup fresh orange juice
	Sea salt, for sprinkling

SERVES 10–12

1 Bring 6 cups water to a boil in a 4-qt. saucepan and add oranges. Return water to a boil and drain. Repeat boiling process twice more with fresh water. Put oranges, 1 cup granulated sugar, and 4 cups water into a 4-qt. saucepan over medium-high. Cook, stirring often, until sugar dissolves and orange rind can be easily pierced with a fork, about 30 minutes. Remove pan from heat and let cool to room temperature.

2 Heat oven to 350°F. Grease a 10″ round cake pan with butter and dust with flour; line pan bottom with parchment paper cut to fit. Set pan aside. Whisk together flour, baking powder, and baking soda in a bowl and set aside. Remove orange quarters from syrup, reserving syrup for another use; remove and discard any seeds from oranges and pulse oranges in a food processor to a chunky purée, 10 to 12 pulses. Add remaining granulated sugar, reserved flour mixture, vanilla, and eggs and process until incorporated, about 2 minutes. Add oil and process until combined. Pour batter into prepared pan and bake until a toothpick inserted in center comes out clean, 40–45 minutes. Let cool for 30 minutes.

3 In a small bowl, whisk confectioners' sugar and orange juice to make a thin glaze. Remove cake from pan and transfer to a cake stand or plate. Using a pastry brush, brush orange glaze over top and sides of cake and let cool completely. Sprinkle cake with salt.

Cooks in the Piedmontese alpine town of Oulx flavor this traditional apple tart, named for the town's patron saint, with red wine and cinnamon. Before the apples are arranged on the pastry, they are simmered in the wine, which turns them a beautiful deep burgundy.

SANT'ANTONIO APPLE TART

2 cups flour, plus more for dusting

7 tbsp. sugar, plus more for sprinkling

1 tsp. baking soda

6 tbsp. cold unsalted butter, cut into ½" cubes

¼ cup milk

2 egg yolks

1¼ cups red wine

¼ tsp. ground cinnamon

¼ tsp. kosher salt

4 Granny Smith apples, peeled, cored, and thinly sliced

Grated zest of 1 orange

1 egg white, lightly beaten

SERVES 8

1 In a bowl, whisk together flour, 1 tbsp. sugar, and baking soda; rub butter into flour until pea-size crumbles form. In another bowl, whisk together milk and egg yolks; using a fork, mix into flour. Transfer to a floured surface and knead into a ball. Cover in plastic wrap and chill for 1 hour.

2 Bring remaining sugar, the wine, cinnamon, salt, apples, and orange zest to a boil in a 4-qt. saucepan. Reduce heat to medium-low and simmer until wine is reduced to a syrup, 25–30 minutes. Let cool.

3 Heat oven to 375°F. Transfer dough to a lightly floured surface and roll out to ⅛" thickness. Transfer dough to an 11" tart pan with a removable bottom and press into bottom and sides. Trim dough edges and reserve scraps. Transfer apple mixture to pan; fold dough sides over edges. To make garnish, roll dough scraps to ⅛" thickness. Cut out leaf and grape shapes and arrange on top of tart. Brush dough with egg white and sprinkle with sugar. Bake until golden, 25–30 minutes. Let cool completely before serving.

The use of cornstarch in this simple gelato base results in a silky-smooth texture. If you like, build flavor by adding puréed fruit or chocolate chips before freezing.

SICILIAN VANILLA GELATO

2¼	cups milk
¾	cup heavy cream
1	vanilla bean, split lengthwise
¾	cup sugar
2	tbsp. cornstarch
1	egg yolk

SERVES 6–8

1 Combine 1¼ cups milk, the cream, and vanilla bean in a 4-qt. saucepan and heat over medium until bubbles appear around edge of pan and mixture is about to boil, 8–10 minutes. Meanwhile, put remaining milk, sugar, and cornstarch in a small bowl and stir until combined. Remove saucepan from heat and stir in cornstarch mixture. Return saucepan to heat and cook, stirring frequently, until sugar has dissolved and mixture has thickened slightly, 8–10 minutes. Remove saucepan from heat.

2 Whisk egg yolk in a bowl until slightly thickened. Gradually whisk 1 cup hot milk mixture into yolk, then gradually return mixture to saucepan, whisking constantly. Set aside to cool, stirring often, then cover with plastic wrap and refrigerate overnight. Remove vanilla bean.

3 Process in an ice cream maker according to manufacturer's directions.

INDEX

TABLE OF EQUIVALENTS

The exact equivalents in the following tables have been rounded for convenience.

Liquid and Dry Measurements

U.S.	METRIC
¼ teaspoon	1.25 milliliters
½ teaspoon	2.5 milliliters
1 teaspoon	5 milliliters
1 tablespoon (3 teaspoons)	15 milliliters
1 fluid ounce	30 milliliters
¼ cup	65 milliliters
⅓ cup	80 milliliters
1 cup	235 milliliters
1 pint (2 cups)	480 milliliters
1 quart (4 cups, 32 fluid ounces)	950 milliliters
1 gallon (4 quarts)	3.8 liters
1 ounce (by weight)	28 grams
1 pound	454 grams
2.2 pounds	1 kilogram

Length Measures

U.S.	METRIC
⅛ inch	3 millimeters
¼ inch	6 millimeters
½ inch	12 millimeters
1 inch	2.5 centimeters

Oven Temperatures

FAHRENHEIT	CELSIUS	GAS
250°	120°	½
275°	140°	1
300°	150°	2
325°	160°	3
350°	180°	4
375°	190°	5
400°	200°	6
425°	220°	7
450°	230°	8
475°	240°	9
500°	260°	10

ACKNOWLEDGMENTS

Many people deserve recognition for their contributions to the making of this cookbook. Chief among them is SAVEUR test kitchen director Farideh Sadeghin, who worked tirelessly to curate existing SAVEUR recipes, develop and test new ones, prepare dishes for photography, and generally help bring this volume to fruition. Also assisting in the kitchen were food editor Ben Mims and test kitchen assistant Jake Cohen—not to mention the many former kitchen staff members and chefs whose recipes made the final cut of our favorite Italian comfort food. On the writing and editing side, thanks go to deputy editor Yaran Noti, senior editors Sophie Brickman and Mari Uyehara, assistant editor Alexander Testere, and a group of writers and interns, including Genevieve Ko, Teri Tsang Barrett, Laura Grahame, and Giancarlo Buonomo. For the visuals in the book, we especially thank SAVEUR photo editor Michelle Heimerman,

staff photographer Matt Taylor-Gross, photographer Joseph DeLeo, and stylist Judy Haubert, along with the many others whose work is represented here. And finally, a special thanks to managing editor Camille Rankin, whose oversight of this project helped us all get to the gate on time.

On the publishing side, we are extremely grateful to our partners at Weldon Owen for their vision and expert handling of this latest book in our ongoing collaboration. Thanks go in particular to Kelly Booth and Marisa Kwek for the beautiful design of the book; to Amy Kaneko and Roger Shaw for bringing it to the consumer; and, most of all, to Amy Marr, for her leadership and unflagging optimism during the inevitable ups and downs of bringing this project to completion.

—Adam Sachs

PHOTOGRAPHY CREDITS

Cover photograph by Marcus Nilsson and food styling by Victoria Granof

Todd Coleman 9, 29, 53, 83, 96, 103, 108, 120, 124, 127, 143, 176, 185, 206; **Joseph De Leo** 1, 14, 42, 60, 65, 69, 104, 123, 130, 134, 138, 144, 149, 152, 157, 163; **Penny De Los Santos** 8, 222; **David Hagerman** 4-5, 223; **Michelle Heimerman** 198, 219; **Ingalls Photography** 95, 116, 158; **Stock Italia/Alamy** 212-213; **Michael Kraus** 113; **John Lee**; 12-13, 40-41, 72-73, 128-129, 166-167, 190-191; **Jason Lowe** 10; **Marcus Nilsson** 2, 107; **Landon Nordeman** 17; **Con Poulos** 74, 77, 78; **Sara Remington** 214; **Farideh Sadeghin** 35, 50, 66, 91, 171, 179, 197; **Laura Sant** 59; **Zoe Schaeffer** 47; **Matt Taylor-Gross** 20, 23, 26, 38, 56, 84, 87, 88, 137, 168, 172, 192, 203; **Michael Turek** 133; **Romulo Yanes** 32, 70, 92, 98-99, 180, 188

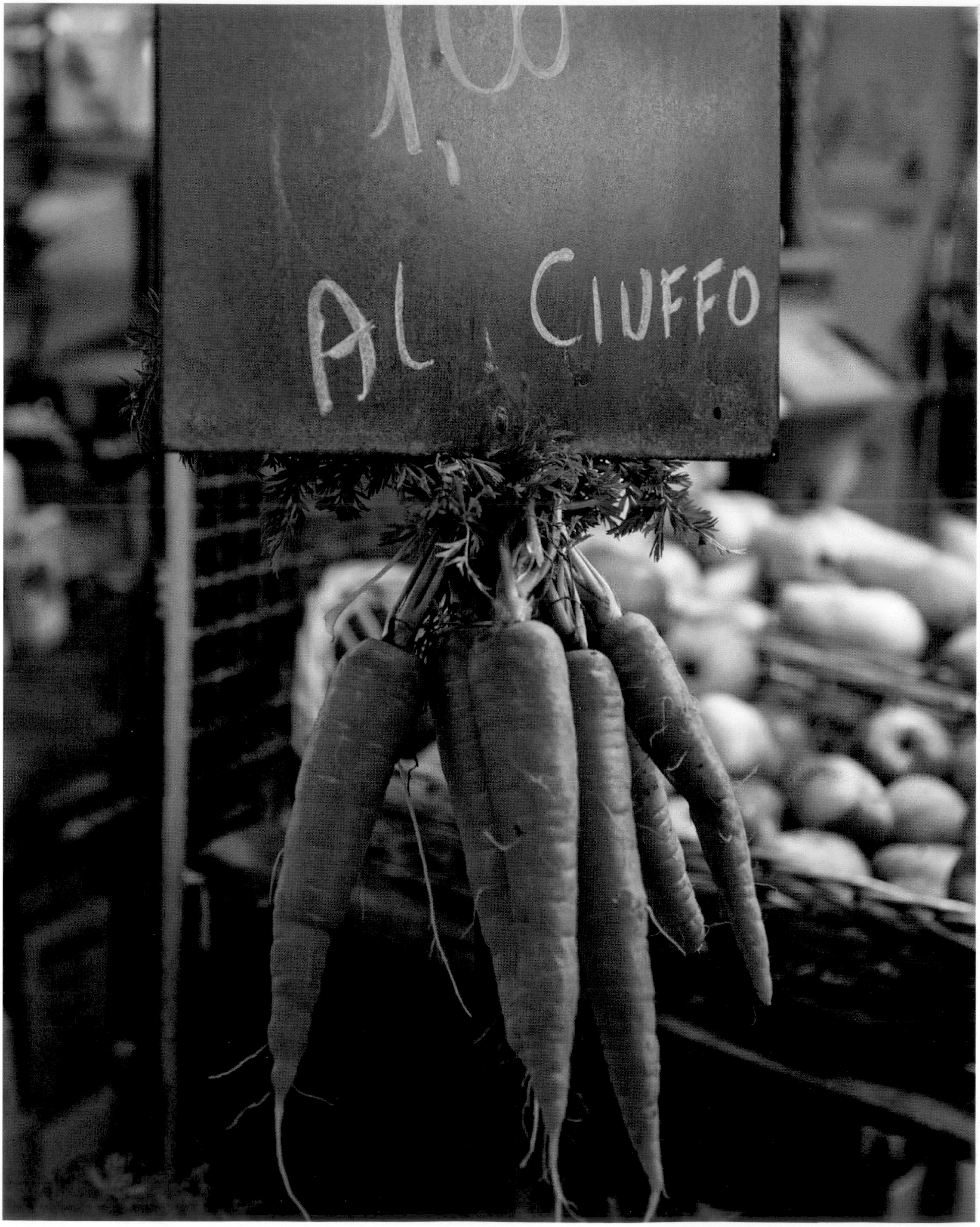
1,00
AL CIUFFO